Sell on Amazon

A Guide to Amazon's Marketplace, Seller Central, and Fulfillment by Amazon Programs

Steve Weber

Sell on Amazon

A Guide to Amazon's Marketplace, Seller Central, and Fulfillment by Amazon Programs

By Steve Weber

Published by Stephen W. Weber
Printed in the United States of America
Weber Books   www.WeberBooks.com

Author: Steve Weber
Editor: Julie Bird

13-digit ISBN: 978-0-9772406-4-7
10-digit ISBN: 0-9772406-4-9

Also by Steve Weber:

eBay 101: Selling on eBay For Part-time or Full-time Income, Beginner to PowerSeller in 90 Days

The Home-Based Bookstore: Start Your Own Business Selling Used Books on Amazon, eBay or Your Own Web Site

Plug Your Book! Online Book Marketing for Authors, Book Publicity through Social Networking

Plug Your Business! Marketing on MySpace, YouTube, blogs and podcasts and other Web 2.0 social networks

Acknowledgments

The following people graciously donated their expertise by reviewing this manuscript and providing corrections, important new information, and crucial perspective:

- **Kevin O'Brien** of Spaceware, a longtime, independent provider of automation software for Amazon sellers. Kevin's daily contact with the Amazon seller community enabled him to provide invaluable assistance with this project. To download a free trial of the company's listing, pricing and order-management software, see:

http://spaceware.com

- **Randy Smythe**, an Amazon seller with the nickname inetmedi-asource, provided unique input from his experience as a high-volume user of Amazon, Fulfillment by Amazon and eBay. Randy regularly provides free advice and important, unique information to sellers on his Web site:

http://www.myblogutopia.com.

Contents

Warning and Disclaimer

The information in this book is offered with the understanding that it does not contain legal, financial, or other professional advice. Individuals requiring such services should consult a competent professional.

The author and publisher make no representations about the suitability of the information contained in this book for any purpose. This material is provided "as is" without warranty of any kind.

Although every effort has been made to ensure the accuracy of the contents of this book, errors and omissions can occur. The publisher assumes no responsibility for any damages arising from the use of this book, or alleged to have resulted in connection with this book.

This book is not completely comprehensive. Some readers may wish to consult additional books for advice.

This book is not authorized or endorsed by Amazon or any other company mentioned in the text.

Introduction

If you're in business to sell consumer goods—or you want to be—you should be on Amazon.com. More than 90 million consumers regularly shop at Amazon, and the number grows daily. As its business has blossomed, Amazon has made it easy for third-party sellers—individuals, large businesses, and mom-and-pop stores—to grab a piece of the action. If you already have a Web or brick-and-mortar store, you can probably boost your volume and profits by showing your wares on Amazon, the world's biggest store.

This book explains the myriad ways that you can profit by partnering with Amazon. Perhaps eBay is more famous for online selling, but today Amazon is the most popular online marketplace, having passed eBay in buyer traffic during the 2007/2008 holiday buying season.

Amazon also ranks among the highest-rated online retailers in customer satisfaction, price, and selection. By selling on Amazon and playing by its rules, you can leverage the Amazon brand name and prime Internet real estate from day one.

Selling on Amazon is big business. Third-party merchants like you and me sell 26 percent of the items sold on Amazon. And that's just fine with Amazon, because its merchants pay commissions on each sale. In return, sellers are rewarded with a steady stream of paying customers, without the traditional risks of retailing. With an Amazon business, you don't need to put up cash for advertising, insurance, employees, retail showrooms, or any of the other major costs of traditional retailing.

Unlike many other large shopping sites, Amazon doesn't charge sellers any fees until your goods have been bought and paid for. And perhaps most importantly, Internet fraud is exceedingly rare at Amazon, in contrast to many Web shopping venues. Amazon screens your customers for you, collects the payments, and sends the proceeds to your bank account.

If you don't want to deal with online buyers yourself, Amazon will handle it all for you. For some extra fees, Amazon will ship your items to customers and handle all customer service, e-mails, and product returns. All you need to do is ship your goods to an Amazon warehouse. (For more information, see the section in this book on "Outsource your Fulfillment.")

Discovering Amazon

Little more than a decade after its founding as an online bookstore, Amazon has evolved into an amazingly effective tool for all sorts of businesses, big and small:

- The existing brick-and-mortar retailer who wants to get additional exposure for his or her products online.

- The startup entrepreneur who wants to start a business selling products from home.

- Anyone with access to new or used consumer items—ranging from books, movies, and electronic gadgets to games or practically anything else—who wants to convert those items into cash quickly and easily.

- Manufacturers or distributors who want additional exposure for their products on the Internet.

- Publishers, liquidators, and others who want to move overstock and "long tail" merchandise. If there's a buyer for your item somewhere in the world, they can find you on Amazon.

- The artisan or inventor who wants to get broader exposure for his or her wares.

If you have something to sell, get it on Amazon, and you'll sell more of it—on Amazon and everywhere else. Amazon's personalized product recommendations can generate sales for you not only on Amazon's Web site, but in local brick-and-mortar stores, too. Millions of shoppers make their buying decisions on Amazon because of the quick, easy access to product information and unbiased consumer reviews, then drive to a local store to pick up an item immediately.

Rest assured, you don't need your own Web site or any special computer expertise to sell on Amazon. If you're comfortable using e-mail, you've got all the skills you need to get started selling on Amazon.

What if you've already got a Web site on which you're selling products, or you're planning one? Read on, and discover how to use Amazon to funnel new and repeat customers to your business.

Get started on Amazon

Amazon Marketplace is a sales platform available to businesses or individuals who sell new, refurbished and collectible products. The offers from these merchants get prominent placement on Amazon's product detail pages, right alongside Amazon's own listins.

For example, when you view Amazon's retail price for an item, nearby you'll see a link such as **36 used & new from $18.99.** Clicking the link brings you to the offer listing page for Amazon's Marketplace sellers. All you need to do to start selling is click the yellow **Sell Yours Here** button. Then you can provide banking details so Amazon can transmit the money from your sales, and you'll choose your business name, also known as a "seller nickname."

Once you're participating as a seller, you can monitor all your activities at your **Seller Account** page:

http://www.amazon.com/seller-account

See the four degrees of Amazon

Amazon has four levels of seller programs:

An individual selling account. Anyone with a regular Amazon consumer account can click the **Sell Yours Here** button on an Amazon product page to offer a used, new or collectible item for sale. There are no listing fees, but Amazon collects a 15 percent commission on each sale plus additional miscellaneous fees.

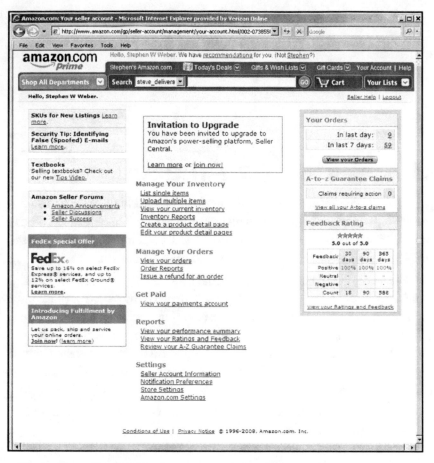

The personalized Seller Account page for Amazon-registered users:
http://www.amazon.com/seller-account

- **Pro-Merchant subscribers.** For $39.99, Amazon provides volume listing and inventory-management tools, and waives the 99-cent per-item fee charged on sales to individual accounts. For sellers who regularly sell more than 40 items per month, the Pro-Merchant subscription is a great deal because it reduces selling costs and allows you to further automate your business.

- **Fulfillment by Amazon.** Instead of selling and shipping items to buyers directly, sellers ship their items to Amazon's warehouse.

For extra fees, Amazon stores the merchandise, handles customer service, and ships the items to the buyer. A big advantage of this program is that your listings qualify for Amazon's various free shipping offers. Buyers of regular Pro-Merchant listings must pay at least a few dollars for shipping—for example, $3.99 for books and $2.98 for CDs and DVDs.

- **Merchants@ Program.** This is a higher level of Pro-Merchant status, sometimes referred to as **Gold- and Platinum-level sellers.** Participating sellers, often large-volume vendors with access to wholesale prices, get extra visibility on Amazon's site. If you're already a Pro-Merchant with a good track record of sales and customer service, you'll probably get an invitation to this program. To apply, visit this contact form and indicate what category of merchandise you're interested in selling:

http://www.amazonservices.com/contactus

List an item on Marketplace

There are virtually no barriers to listing an item for sale on Amazon Marketplace. If you already have an Amazon consumer account, you can use that account to list items for sale.

To list an item, simply search for the Amazon page for the product you're offering, and click the link **Sell Yours Here.** Amazon's Web site will prompt you for the additional information required for selling privileges.

To search for products, look for the search box at the top of any Amazon page. Search for the item using the product name, title or ISBN or UPC. These are the digits above the barcode on a retail page, and stand for International Standard Book Number or Universal Product Code.

You can also list items from your Seller Account page by clicking the link **Sell single items.**

Beware of restricted products

In addition to preventing the sale of illegal products, Amazon also restricts the sale of certain high-value goods. Sellers of these expensive items must be pre-approved by Amazon, including:

- Computers

- Cell phones (without service) and wireless accessories

Also, sales of certain top-selling items are restricted to pre-approved merchants in these store categories:

- Computer and video games

- Electronics

- Software

Amazon classifies computer games as a subcategory of its Software store, and restricts computer game sales to pre-approved sellers.

Also, Amazon usually restricts the entry of new merchants into its Toys category in the weeks leading up to the holiday buying season. And some stores are simply closed to third-party sellers, including:

- Jewelry

- Watches

- Apparel

- Shoes

Describe your item's condition

Amazon's Web site shows a drop-down menu of condition classifications depending on what type of merchandise you're selling. Here you indicate the item's condition and add comments further describing the item. For example, if you were selling a used DVD, you might classify its condition as "Good" and add the comments: "Has rental-store sticker and light scratches."

Designating condition and your description. Take pains to describe items accurately, and disclose all defects. Err on the side of caution. Accuracy in descriptions boosts buyer satisfaction, your repeat business, and your feedback ratings from customers.

Rate your items' condition

You can sell items in any of four condition categories on Amazon: New, Used, Collectible, and for certain types of products, Refurbished. It's important to accurately grade your items because your customer satisfaction and reputation depend on it.

Amazon has fairly precise guidelines for rating new or used products on Amazon:

- **New:** A brand-new, unused, unopened product in its original packaging and with all original packaging materials included. The original manufacturer's warranty, if any, should still apply, with details of the warranty included in your condition comments.

- **Like New:** An apparently untouched product, in perfect condition. The original plastic wrap may be missing, but the original packaging is intact and pristine, and instructions are included. There are absolutely no signs of wear. Suitable for presenting as a gift.

- **Very Good:** A well-preserved item that has seen limited use but remains in excellent condition. The item is complete, unmarked, and undamaged, but may show some limited signs of wear. The product works perfectly.

- **Good:** The product shows wear from consistent use, but remains in good condition. The item may be marked or have identifying information on it, and show other signs of previous use. The product works perfectly.

- **Refurbished:** The product was professionally restored to working order. This usually means the item was cleaned, inspected and repaired according to manufacturer specifications. The original packaging might not be included. A manufacturer's warranty—or a warranty of the company that refurbished it—should apply and be explained in the condition comments.

- **Acceptable:** The product is fairly worn, but it continues to work perfectly. The signs of wear can include scratches, dents, and other aesthetic problems. The product may be marked or have identifying information on it, and may show other signs of previous use.

- **Unacceptable:** Products that do not work perfectly in every regard are unacceptable, and thus ineligible for selling on Amazon. Items that are damaged in ways that render them difficult to use are likewise unacceptable. Items for which essential accompanying material is missing are unacceptable. Products that require repair or service are unacceptable.

For more detailed guidelines for books, music, videos, electronics, cameras, and other Amazon product lines, consult this Amazon guide:

http://www.amazon.com/gp/help/customer/display.html?no deId=1161242

An offer listing page on Amazon Marketplace. Individuals and large or small businesses can offer new, used or collectible items for sale. To get here, customers click on <u>More Buying Choices, X used & new</u> on Amazon product pages.

Set your price

Now that you've rated the condition of your merchandise, you'll need to decide at what price you want to sell your items, and register to collect payment from Amazon Payments. Amazon collects the money from your buyer's credit card or checking account and deposits it to your Amazon Payments account, where you can transfer the funds to your own bank account once every 24 hours. All customer registration and fraud prevention is handled by Amazon. This contrasts with other sites such as eBay, where sellers often collect their payments by accepting checks or money orders through the mail, or online through PayPal, a payment service owned by eBay.

You can price your items at any price ranging from 1 cent up to $2,500. To maximize your profits and compete for as many sales as possible, you'll want to price your items near the lowest price listed by competitors selling items at the same condition as yours. You don't necessarily have to offer the absolute lowest price to get the sale. As a practical matter, if Amazon carries the same item you're selling, you'll need to beat Amazon's price to get a prompt sale. Don't forget to figure in the fees and commissions you must pay Amazon for the sale, which can exceed 20 percent. You'll receive a shipping credit from Amazon, although it might not cover all your costs for shipping, handling, and packing materials.

Set shipping locations, other options

Depending on the ZIP Code you enter, your listing on Amazon will show the location you're shipping from, which gives buyers a general idea of the distance involved. You must decide whether to offer expedited or international shipping. These two options can attract more buyers, but again, weigh your costs carefully. If your item is oversized or heavy, your shipping costs may exceed the shipping credit you receive from Amazon. In this case, you'll want to increase your selling price, or not offer expedited or international shipping for your item.

Collectibles. Items such as special editions or autographed merchandise can be designated "Collectible" and may sell at a premium compared with the regular retail price. You're free to set your price as you see fit, as long as you adhere to a few general guidelines. According to Amazon's general pricing rule, only items priced at or above the manufacturer's list price (MSRP) or $10, whichever is greater, are eligible for the Collectible designation.

Amazon General Pricing Rule: Amazon policy dictates that you give Amazon buyers your best deal, According to Marketplace rules, the price of your item on Amazon must be equal to or below the price you're offering anywhere else. So if you sell an item for $10 in a retail store, on eBay or elsewhere, Amazon expects you to sell it at the same or lower price on Amazon, including shipping. In other words, the total bill for one of your customers on Amazon—the item price, plus shipping and handling fees, minus any discounts or rebates—must match or beat the deal you're offering anywhere else.

Although these are Amazon's rules on pricing, many sellers are unaware of many of the details. As a practical matter, with millions of items listed and constantly repriced by thousands of its sellers, it's hard to imagine how Amazon could ensure compliance with this policy.

Set quantity and SKU

In the retail trade, this stands for Stock Keeping Unit and is used to identify particular items being sold. You can use the SKU system to help automate your inventory system. The SKU you assign to each of your products can be numbers, letters or a combination.

SKUs are mandatory at Amazon. If you have an individual selling account, Amazon generates the SKU for you. If you have a Pro-Merchant subscription, you can specify the SKU, or allow Amazon to generate SKUs for you by leaving the SKU field blank.

If you have multiple copies of the same item in the same condition, you should insert that numeral in the **Quantity** box on the listing form instead of creating separate listings for each item. Otherwise the default quantity is one.

Amazon allows no more than five identical listings in a category. However, if you have multiple copies of the same item, in different conditions—such as New, Good, or refurbished—you should create a separate listing for each item.

An offer listing page on Amazon Marketplace. Individuals or businesses can offer new, used or collectible items for sale. Customers arrive here by clicking More Buying Choices, X used & new on product pages.

Take Amazon Payments

Amazon processes all the payments for sales made on its site. Amazon doesn't allow telephone orders or permit customers to mail in checks or money orders. Nor may customers use a third-party payment service such as PayPal. Instead, all customers pay for their purchases using **Amazon Payments**, and sellers receive the proceeds via electronic bank transfer. Sellers also have the option of receiving their funds in the form of an Amazon gift certificate, an option used by some low-volume and nonprofit sellers.

Applying for Amazon Payments is a requirement for selling on Amazon. If you haven't signed up yet, you'll be prompted to apply when you list your first item for sale. You'll need to have a check handy so you can specify your bank account and routing numbers. You can initiate a funds transfer once every 24 hours, or you can wait for Amazon to automatically transfer the funds in two-week intervals. Amazon handles fraud prevention, and there are no fees for using Amazon Payments; all the costs are included in Amazon's Marketplace commission structure.

Buyers who purchase using Amazon Payments receive money-back guarantee coverage up to $2,500 under a program known as Amazon's A-to-Z Guarantee.

Amazon Payments on third-party sites. Participating merchants can also accept Amazon Payments on non-Amazon Web sites by using a "Pay Now" button. The button is a simple bit of computer code—known as an HTML widget—that allows merchants to collect payments on their blog or Web site. For more information:

https://payments.amazon.com/sdui

Web site developers also can install a more customized payment process known as Amazon's Flexible Payments Service (FPS):

http://www.amazon.com/b?ie=UTF8&node=342430011

Pay fees and commissions

You'll pay Amazon fees and commissions after your items sell; the amounts are automatically deducted from the buyer's payment. Amazon collects your sales price and a standard shipping fee depending on the type of item. Commissions range from of 6 percent to 15 percent depending on the type of merchandise. In addition, sellers pay per-transaction "closing fees" of 99 cents, and a "variable closing fee." However, the 99-cent per-transaction fee is waived for Pro-Merchant sellers.

Commission rates are as follows:

Automotive Parts	12%
Baby	15%
Camera and Photo	8%
Consumer Electronics	8%
Everything Else	15%
Health & Personal Care	15%
Home and Garden	15%

Musical Instruments	12%
Office Products	15%
Software	15%
Sports and Outdoors	15%
Tools and Hardware	12%
Toys and Games	15%
Video Games	15%
All other product lines	15 %

Variable Closing Fees Charged to Seller:

Unsold listings expire after 60 days for individual Marketplace sellers, and no fees are incurred. Amazon confirms via e-mail that the listing ended, and instructions are giving for relisting the item. By contrast, listings from Pro-Merchant sellers remain active until they sell or the Pro-Merchant subscription is canceled.

In rare cases, Amazon charges fees for poor seller performance, but such circumstances usually apply in cases where the seller account is badly mismanaged. The offenses to trigger such fees are typically excessive refunds, frequent A-to-Z Guarantee claims against a seller, and credit-card chargebacks initiated by buyers.

Identify your products

Most of the products listed for sale on Amazon are identified by a manufacturer's product code such as a Universal Product Code (UPC), International Standard Book Number (ISBN), or European Article Number (EAN). These unique series of digits or numerals can be used to identify the exact item you're selling, and to make the listing process go faster. For example, to list a book for sale on Amazon, you might first search for its product page by searching for the title and author name. But a much faster way to locate the page is to type the book's ISBN, a 10- or 13-digit code usually found above a barcode on the book's back cover.

As you further develop your business on Amazon, these product identifiers will save you even more time. For example, instead of typing each product ID manually, you could attach a barcode scanner to your computer to generate the code automatically.

Closing fees charged for Amazon categories

Shipping mode	Standard	Expedited	International
Books	$1.35	$1.35	$1.35
Music	$0.80	$0.80	$0.80
Videos	$0.80	$0.80	$0.80
DVDs	$0.80	$0.80	$0.80
Video Games (VHS)	$1.35	$1.35	Not available
Software & Computer Games	$1.35	$1.35	Not available
Electronics	$0.45 + $0.05/lb.	$0.65 + $0.10/lb.	Not available
Camera & Photo	$0.45 + $0.05/lb.	$0.65 + $0.10/lb.	Not available
Tools & Hardware	$0.45 + $0.05/lb.	$0.65 + $0.10/lb.	Not available
Kitchen & Housewares	$0.45 + $0.05/lb.	$0.65 + $0.10/lb.	Not available
Outdoor Living	$0.45 + $0.05/lb.	$0.65 + $0.10/lb.	Not available
Computer	$0.45 + $0.05/lb.	$0.65 + $0.10/lb.	Not available
Sports & Outdoors	$0.45 + $0.05/lb.	$0.65 + $0.10/lb.	Not available
Cell phones and accessories	$0.45 + $0.05/lb.	$0.65 + $0.10/lb.	Not available
Musical Instruments	$0.45 + $0.05/lb.	$0.65 + $0.10/lb.	Not available
Office Products	$0.45 + $0.05/lb.	$0.65 + $0.10/lb.	Not available
Toy & Baby	$0.45 + $0.05/lb.	$0.65 + $0.10/lb.	Not available
Everything Else	$0.45 + $0.05/lb	$0.65 + $0.10/lb.	Not available

Items can be further identified on Amazon with a code known as the Amazon Standard Identification Number (ASIN). For example, books printed before the 1970s usually don't have an ISBN, so Amazon assigns its own ASIN to the product page. In other cases, authors who publish their own books—or artisans who list their own creations such as dolls or artwork for sale on Amazon—can create a product detail page for the item and have Amazon assign an ASIN.

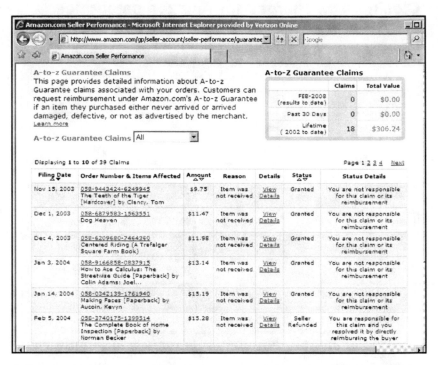

Sellers can monitor A-to-Z Guarantee claims when buyers file for refunds through Amazon.

UPCs. When entering a UPC, be sure to include the smaller numbers on the left and right sides of the bar code. UPCs are located below the bar code:

ISBNs. The numbers representing a book's ISBN can be found above the barcode on the back cover. (Books produced before the late 1970s often have no barcode or ISBN.)

Until recent years the ISBN system consisted of 10-digit codes, but was expanded in 2007 to 13-digit codes because the 10-digit codes were being exhausted. The ISBN-13 is also known as a Bookland EAN and is a subset of the EAN system.

A barcode for the 13-digit ISBN 9780977240630.

Don't include hyphens when entering these numbers on Amazon's selling form. However, if a 10-digit or 13-digit ISBN has an X at the end, include the letter.

EANs. Don't include the dashes between any of the 13 digits in an EAN, which is found below the bar code:

Sometimes you won't be able to find a page on Amazon matching your product identifier because Amazon only includes a product's latest model or edition. In this case, you wouldn't be able to list your item, even though a nearly identical item may appear on Amazon.

Amazon Standard Identification Numbers (ASINs) are often used when there isn't a standardized UPC or ISBN assigned to a product. You can find the ASIN on the item's product page at Amazon.com under the heading **Product Details.** Another way to find a product's ASIN is to look in the browser address bar. Look for the sequence of characters appearing after the item's name and the letters **dp:**

Global Trade Item Numbers (GTINs) are universal identifiers used for identifying products across different databases such as ISBNs, UPCs, EANs, and JANs (Japanese Article Numbers).

GTIN codes resemble the following:

ISBN (old): 10 digits
ISBN-13 (new): 13 digits
UPC: 12 digits
EAN: 13 digits
JAN: 13 digits
ASIN: 10 characters (letters and numbers)

Manage inventory

Each time you list an item on Amazon, you'll receive an e-mail from Amazon confirming the listing, and another message each time the status of a listing changes—such as when a listing becomes active or has been sold. Later, if you decide to further automate your business with order-management software, you'll be able to turn off these e-mail alerts.

Normally your Marketplace listings will show up in Amazon searches and browse categories just a few moments after you've submitted them. They should also appear in your Seller Account within several minutes of submission, although you may have to refresh the Web page before they become visible.

The "Open Listings" page in an Amazon Seller Account. To navigate here, click "View your current inventory" from your Seller Account.

Now that you have active listings on Amazon, you'll need to maintain them, occasionally reviewing the prices against competitors and ensuring your inventory counts are accurate. Here's how:

1. From your Seller Account, click **View your current inventory** to see **Your Marketplace Open Listings**.
2. From here, you can click edit to change the quantity or price of any listing. However, if you need to change the condition (from "Very Good" to "Acceptable," for example) you'll need to close the listing and relist.
3. Review your changes and click **Submit your listing.** If something must still be fixed, click the **Edit** button.

Search and sort your listings

You can also check the box to **Close Listing** at any time before the item is purchased, and there is no fee for doing so. Click the **Save changes** button to make your changes effective.

To look up a particular listing, you can search your listing by various parameters. If you wish, you can sort the display of your listings by several criteria, including listing date, or how your price compares against competing sellers. To change the display, click **Set Your Preferences** from your Open Listings page.

You can also click a listing ID to go directly to the offer detail page, where you'll see the lowest-priced offers by Marketplace sellers.

From the Open Listings page, you can search your listing by these criteria:

- Product Name
- Merchant SKU
- Listing ID
- ASIN/ISBN

Searches for product names aren't case-sensitive, and a partial product name is sufficient. For example, searching for "potter" would locate your listing for "Harry Potter and the Sorcerer's Stone." However, the order of the words your use is important—you'll find the same item in your listing by searching for "harry potter," but not "potter harry." When you search using a product identification number or SKU, you must enter the entire number correctly—partial ISBNs, ASINs or SKUs will not return a search result.

Sort your listings. You can also sort listings by SKU, product name, date submitted, quantity, and price. To sort by these criteria, click on the column heading. For example, to sort by quantity, click the heading **Qty**, and your listings will be displayed with the lowest quantities first. To reverse the order, click on **Qty** again.

Reprice your listings

The Open Listings page has a handy **Low Price** feature enabling you to compare your prices with prices offered by competing sellers, and you can reprice your listings as you see fit. This feature gives you three options for comparing your listings to competing sellers:

1. Compare your listings to **all** listings for the same product, regardless of condition.
2. Compare your listings to listings in the **same condition** (New, Used, Collectible, or Refurbished).
3. Compare your listings to listings in the **same subcondition** (for example, New versus Used - Like New, Used - Very Good, etc.).

A blue checkmark will be displayed by your listings that have the low price according to your preferences. (Make adjustments by clicking **Set your preferences** from the Open Listings page.

Q&A: How often should I reprice?

QUESTION: How often should I reprice my inventory? I used to do it every two or three months, then monthly. Now I do it every two weeks, and I still don't know what interval is best.

I usually drop my price to a penny below the lowest listing matching my item's condition. What have you found to be the ideal timing?

ANSWER: It depends on the type of merchandise you have, your situation, and your business philosophy, which can change over time.

No seller likes to lower their price, but sometimes it's necessary to make a prompt sale. Amazon's Marketplace is a reverse auction. We sellers are competing to offer the best prices and attract the customer.

The average buyer purchasing an inexpensive item looks at only the lowest two or three prices. Savvy buyers and those purchasing more expensive items tend to be more careful. A good feedback record can save you from having to constantly compete only on price. But if your price is too far from the lowest, you're not even going to appear on the first listing page. Few buyers click through to subsequent listing pages.

How often you're motivated to reprice might depend on your cash-flow situation and the number of items in your inventory. At one point, I repriced at least once a day, usually twice. Nowadays I probably re-price once every couple of months. Sometimes I sell my items at a higher price because I haven't chased a downward spiral in prices—and the market price eventually comes back up to where I've been sitting. On the other hand, sometimes my items become totally worthless—and maybe I could have gotten a sale, but now I have junk that will never sell.

Some sellers are obsessed with always having the lowest price, so their listing appears on top of the Marketplace offer page. It's not necessary for you to undercut the lowest price to move your listing to the top; you merely need to match the lowest price.

An automated repricing tool can save an enormous amount of time required by this chore. During my first couple of years selling on Amazon I had 15,000 unique items in my Marketplace inventory, and repricing through Amazon took three entire days. Now, thanks to the software I use, repricing takes about 10 minutes. (See the chapter in this book titled "Kick it Up a Notch.")

Sometimes I use automated repricing for items worth less than $10 or $20, but I usually take the time to individually consider price changes for higher-priced items. The higher the price, the more likely the buyer will consider factors other than price—like feedback. Especially for these pricier items, you need to go with your gut instinct: Will demand for the item probably rise, or fall? Will supply become glutted, or will the item become rare? The longer you've been selling on Amazon, the better you'll be able to predict future demand.

My hunch is it probably doesn't hurt to lower your price a penny or so at a time to keep your visibility on Amazon's offer page—as long as it doesn't eat up other time that you could be devoting to getting new stock, etc.

However, by lowering by "a penny or so at a time," I don't think it's smart to use software to lower your price several times a day. For example, one afternoon I was watching the price of a used book on Marketplace, a book that normally sells for about $18. There were two sellers battling to have the lowest price. They were lowering their price by 6 cents each time—every several minutes! It was automated repricing run amok. The point is, over the course of an afternoon they chased the price down almost $3 until one of the copies sold. The price went right back up, so one of those seller left $3 on the table.

Your pricing philosophy might depend on what kind of items you're selling, or your cost structure. You might have a different pricing philosophy for different parts of your inventory. If you're selling new items you're obtaining wholesale, you only have a certain profit margin for wiggle room. But if you're selling unique items you've obtained cheaply—used books, CDs, videos—you can afford to be more aggressive. With used items, you'll find that about 25 percent of your new inventory sells within the first month. Perhaps another 10 percent sells during the next month. After that, that part of your stock will move slower and slower—you're ending up with a high percentage of deadwood items that nobody is shopping for. That is why some sellers aggressively reprice their used merchandise after it has been on hand more than six months. At some point, that non-moving merchandise begins costing you precious shelf space and storage costs. The Amazon Sales Rank of an item gives you some indication of how quickly an item is likely to sell.

Sometimes, repricing often reveals products in your inventory that are priced too low. Perhaps other sellers have sold out or raised their prices. If you can identify these mispriced items in your inventory quickly, it will fatten your profits.

Excerpted from Steve Weber's "Selling Books" blog.

Edit your listings

If you want to change your prices, you can edit listings one by one, or in bulk using **Manage Your Inventory** tools within your Seller Account.

For example, let's imagine you want to amend the description of one of your listings. After locating the listing, click **Edit** in the right-hand column, and you can change the text of your description. From here, you can also edit the item's price and change the shipping methods you're offering.

Changing the condition of a Marketplace item, however, will require closing the current listing and making a new one.

Edit listings in bulk. In your Seller Account, you can amend the quantity or price for multiple items by changing the numbers in the Price or Quantity columns. After making your changes, click **Save Changes.** If you decide to abandon your changes, click **Reset Values**.

You may close listings in bulk by checking the **Close Listing** box in the appropriate column for each item you want to close. After making your selections, click **Save Changes.**

Relist your items

For sellers with a regular Amazon account, listings expire after 60 days, and can by relisted manually from the Open Listings page. Listings for Pro-Merchants remain available until the item or complete quantity is sold.

Sold Listings. Your Closed Listings page shows listings that have been canceled, sold, or expired. To find the shipping information for sold listings, click **Manage Your Orders** from your Seller Account.

Managing large inventories. As a practical matter, managing a large inventory on Amazon requires a Pro-Merchant subscription. Pro-Merchant status provides access to special inventory tools, enabling bulk uploading and repricing using a database or text file. Also, Amazon waives the 99-cent per-transaction closing fee for Pro-Merchants. So if you're selling more than 40 items per month on Marketplace, the Pro-

Merchant subscription is a great deal. Pro-Merchant status also entitles you to create a page for a new product currently not listed on Amazon.

Manage inventory the smart way

- Manage your inventory on a daily basis by using Amazon's inventory loading tools to make regular additions and deletions.

- Use Amazon's pre-built Price & Quantity template to make quick changes to prices or quantities of existing inventory.

- Add new inventory and modify or delete existing inventory using the pre-built Inventory Loader and Book Loader templates, or a UIEE (Universal Information Exchange Environment) file.

- For smoother uploads, break large Inventory Loader files into small batches.

- After your file finishes processing, review the error log.

- If you need to quickly remove all of your listings, upload an Inventory Loader file with all column headers but with no listings, and select the Purge and Replace option before uploading.

- Review the file formatting requirements prior to uploading on the Amazon site.

- Always use unique SKUs that relate only to one particular product; don't reuse the same SKU for a different product.

Reconcile your inventory

No matter how well you manage your inventory and Amazon listings, soon or later something will get out of whack. Here are two methods for finding discrepancies between your Amazon listings and the inventory you have on hand, assuming you are a Pro-Merchant subscriber:

- **Generate an Open Listings Report.** You'll find the link for this report in your Seller Account. By comparing your open listings report to your current on-hand inventory, you can determine which Marketplace listings need to be modified, deleted, or added.

- **Use a backup.** Maintain a list of your Amazon listings on your computer to double-check your Open Listings report.

Removing your listings. There are two ways to make all your Amazon listings unavailable. On a temporary basis, you could put your Seller Account "on vacation" by activating this feature from the link on your Seller Account page. Alternatively, if you're a Pro-Merchant you could upload a "Purge and Replace" file that includes all the Inventory Loader column headers, but no listings.

Upload inventory files to Amazon

For Pro-Merchants, Amazon accepts two different kinds of tab-delimited Inventory Loader formats. Column headers should be all lower-case letters.

- A file built from an Inventory Loader template, Standard Book Loader Template, or a UIEE file. (UIEE stands for Universal Information Exchange Environment, an inventory format commonly used in the book industry).

- A Price & Quantity Template, which can be used only for Modify/Delete uploads. May contain a maximum of three columns: SKU (required), price (optional) and Quantity (optional). The Modify/Delete format enables you to delete items by simply entering a zero in the "Quantity" field for that SKU and uploading the file.

For more information, see Amazon's help section on volume selling:

http://www.amazon.com/gp/help/customer/display.html?ie= UTF8&nodeId=1161306

Use SKUs

If you have a large inventory, your bookkeeping will be easier to manage by using SKUs, or Stock Keeping Units.

Assign an SKU to each listing to identify it uniquely. SKUs can be up to 40 characters long and can be letters and numbers or a combination.

SKUs must be unique because Amazon doesn't allow duplicate SKUs. And you shouldn't reuse an SKU for a new product because this can cause confusion with your inventory.

One good way to manage SKUs is to employ a combination of letters plus the ISBN or UPC of the product. This method works when managing multiple inventories with one account or listing the same product under different condition classifications.

Here's an example of how SKUs can work for medium-sized and larger sellers. Let's imagine your Amazon inventory is physically housed in your basement on a shelving unit with five stacked shelves. You could fashion an SKU system by assigning a letter to each shelf and a numeral to each item on that shelf. For example, the SKUs on the top shelf would be A-1, A-2, A-3 and so on. On the next shelf down, the item SKUs would be B-1, B-2, B-3, and so on. Later on, as your inventory expands to dozens more shelving units, this simple SKU system can save valuable time when you're picking and packing items in response to customer orders.

Now let's imagine an SKU system on a larger scale. Let's say a seller wants to list inventory from two separate shops or storage areas. The seller could handle this by assigning a SKU prefix to each store, such as A for Store 1 and B for Store 2. So this seller's SKUs could be A-A1, A-A2, B-A1, B-A2, and so on.

Secure your Amazon account

You should avoid logging into your Amazon account on public computers, such as those in a library. And beware of bogus e-mails that appear to be from Amazon, but may have been sent by a computer hacker. These bogus messages are also known as "spoof" messages or "phishing" messages. These messages urge you to reveal your account ID and password, and often contain a link that looks like a legitimate link to Amazon.

Unfortunately, these spoof Web sites can be used by hackers to steal your account details and commit fraud using your Amazon account.

Here are some basic guidelines for protecting yourself against hackers and phishers. Amazon.com will never send an e-mail asking you for the following information:

- Your Amazon password.

- Your Social Security number or tax identification number.

- Your bank account information, credit card number, PIN number, or credit card security code.

- Mother's maiden name or other information to identify you, such as birth city or name of a pet.

Another way to recognize bogus messages is to look for typographical errors and poor grammar. Many of these hoax messages are translated from another language and aren't proofread. Also, check the return address for the e-mail. Does the e-mail address end in **@amazon.com**? If not, it's a hoax message.

Does the message contain a link to an authentic Amazon Web page, or something else? A spoof Web site may contain the word "amazon" somewhere in the URL, but genuine Amazon pages always end with "amazon.com."

Best practices

Amazon prescribes these "best practices" for account security:

- Change your password regularly.

- Consider setting up a separate bank account for disbursements from your Amazon Payments account.

- Amazon.com never asks you to verify sensitive information via e-mail. Submit such information only when completing an order on our Web site, registering for Amazon Payments, or contacting Amazon directly through its Web forms.

- Review the terms of Amazon's online privacy notice.

View and search your orders

Amazon sends you an e-mail notification when an item sells and posts the order in your seller account. To look at your orders, go to your Seller Account page and click **View your orders.**

Order History - Amazon Services Order Notifier

File   Edit   Help

Display orders received within: 30 days ▾ 🔄 Check Now ⬚ Settings... ❓

Event Date	Items	Total	Title
9:42 AM	1	$4.79	Wallpaper City Guide: Istanbul (Wallpaper City ...
9:42 AM	**1**	**$12.05**	**Deep Storm: A Novel [Hardcover] by ...**
9:41 AM	1	$37.26	Game Programming Gems 6 (Book & C...
9:41 AM	1	$39.85	Public Key Infrastructure: Building Trusted Appli...
9:40 AM	1	$10.83	Baby the Rain Must Fall/It's Gonna Be Fine [Au...
9:40 AM	**1**	**$23.51**	**Modal Logic for Philosophers [Paperba...**
9:39 AM	2	$15.94	Fiesta Black 494 7-Inch Covered Butter Dish [K...
9:39 AM	1	$6.10	The Westminster Shorter Catechism: For Study ...
9:39 AM	**1**	**$12.37**	**CLEP German (w/audio CD) (College-L...**
9:38 AM	1	$7.43	Let's Wiggle [Audio CD] The Wiggles
9:38 AM	1	$12.55	Farberware Select 8-Inch and 10-Inch Skillets, ...
9:38 AM	1	$23.10	Debating Political Reform in China: Rule of Law...
9:37 AM	1	$38.27	Paul Wilmott Introduces Quantitative Finance [...
9:37 AM	1	$19.54	Kaplan TOEFL iBT with CD-ROM, 2007-2008 ...
9:37 AM	1	$62.46	Family Therapy: A Systemic Integration (6th Edi...
9:37 AM	1	$7.52	Yellowbeard [DVD] (2006) Graham Chapman; ...
9:37 AM	1	$69.79	The Way of the Dreamer with Robert Moss [DV...

4 unviewed orders Last Updated: 2 Mar 2007, 9:42 AM

Amazon's ASON software lets you view recent orders.

After clicking on **View Your** Orders, you'll see a list of your recent orders. You can view the buyer's shipping address and other order information by clicking on the **Order Id** link. On the Manage Orders page, you'll find the shipping address, listing ID, SKU, and payment total. From this page, you can print a packing slip and shipping label or issue a refund for part or all of the order.

Search for a specific order. From the Seller Account page, click **View your orders** to navigate to the Manage Orders page. Here you may search for a particular order by several criteria: listing ID, order number, or buyer e-mail address. You can also search for orders by the product name or SKU. To search for multiple orders, enter a product name or SKU and select a date range.

Your search results are shown as a list with the transaction date, order ID, and buyer e-mail.

Amazon Services Order Notifier. As an alternative to viewing your orders on Amazon's Web site, the company provides an optional Windows desktop application known as ASON. The software runs in the background, periodically polling Amazon to retrieve new orders. You'll be notified of new orders by a pop-up window. ASON holds your order history of the past 30 days, to a maximum of 5,000 orders.

ASON enables you to view the details of each order and print shipping labels and packing slips.

For more information about downloading and installing ASON, visit this page:

http://www.amazon.com/gp/help/customer/display.html?ie= UTF8&nodeId=200121270

Create a product detail page

If you have a product that isn't already listed in Amazon's catalog, you can create an Amazon product page for it, so long as you're a Pro-Merchant subscriber.

Seller-created detail pages are currently allowed in these categories:

- Baby
- Books
- Camera & Photo
- Computer & Video Games
- Electronics

Order Detail

Order information

Order ID	058-1111111-1111111	View orders in Your Seller Account
Listings:	1	
Items:	1	

Mastery: The Keys to Success a ... $5.75   1
SKU: 37:LEX1:ZZZZZFJKDFJKSDFJKJ
Order-item ID: 65465465465465
Condition: 4-2
Condition Note: Amazon.com subsidiary with same five sta ...

Shipping information

Buyer name: Joe Smith
Buyer e-mail: joesmith@mail.com
Time of sale: 18 Dec 2006 5:02 PM (PST)
Shipping speed: Standard

[Print shipping label & packing slip]

(Please note Media mail should only be user for standard shipping in Books, Music, Videos, DVDs, Computer Games, Video Games, and Computer Software.)

Transaction information

Buyer price:	$5.75	Learn more about transaction information
Amazon commission:	($0.86)	
Additional shipping credit:	$0.00	
Your Earnings:	**$8.38**	

[Close]

ASON's order detail screen.

- Kitchen, Home & Garden
- Music
- Musical Instruments
- Pet Supplies
- Software
- Sporting Goods
- Tools & Hardware
- Toys & Games
- Video & DVD
- Everything Else

You can search or browse for your product's category using Amazon's "create a product detail page" feature.

Sellers aren't allowed to create detail pages in other categories, but Amazon plans to loosen these restrictions in the coming years. Items that aren't prohibited but don't fit an existing Amazon category may be listed in the "Everything Else" category.

Product identifiers such as ISBNs and UPCs are required to sell items in some categories. For example, UPCs are required for items listed in Amazon's Music, Video, DVD, Video Games, Software, Electronics,

Kitchen & Housewares, or Camera & Photo categories. ISBNs aren't required when creating a page in the Books category. However, duplicate detail pages aren't permitted, and if a book has an ISBN, you must provide it when creating a detail page for the book.

To create a product detail page on Amazon, visit this page and follow the instructions:

http://selection.amazon.com/abis/Classify/DisplayClassify.a mzn

For a step-by-step walk through of the detail page creation process, visit this page on Amazon:

http://www.amazon.com/gp/help/customer/display.html?ie= UTF8&nodeId=10524331

Amazon velocity limits

To prevent fraud by disreputable sellers, Amazon imposes "velocity limits" to restrict how quickly sellers may accept payments from buyers. At certain points along the way, Amazon wants to ensure the seller has successfully filled most of its orders. Assuming the seller has not canceled too many orders or issued excessive refunds, Amazon routinely raises the seller's velocity limit.

Seller velocity limits are applied throughout a 28-day rolling period. The initial velocity limit is set automatically at the time of registration, and can vary from seller to seller. Your first limit may be a few thousand dollars. If Amazon has trouble verifying any of the information you provided during your registration, you may have a lower initial velocity limit.

Amazon's velocity limits operate on the same principle as the fraud-detection efforts of banks and credit-card issuers. For example, if you charge $10,000 on your Visa card this weekend, you'll likely receive a phone call from your card company on Monday morning. They'll want to ensure your card hasn't been stolen. Similarly, Amazon wants to prevent crooks and scammers from using an Amazon selling account.

Each time you approach your velocity limit, you'll receive an automated e-mail from Amazon asking you to reply with your full name and telephone number. Usually your velocity limit is raised within a day or two.

Velocity limits can be increased at any time. However, if you're approaching or have exceeded your current limit, Amazon might block further sales until your limit is raised.

If Amazon approves an increase to your velocity limit, any pending orders will be allowed to proceed. If the increase is denied, pending orders are canceled until old sales drop off your 28-day cycle. Amazon can also decrease your velocity limit if something appears suspicious with your account.

Amazon also limits the size of individual transactions on Marketplace. The maximum dollar amount the company will process for any individual transaction is $2,475.

If you have a question about your velocity limit, send an e-mail to payments-request@amazon.com.

Best practices

Amazon prescribes these "best practices" for Marketplace listings and management of inventory and orders:

- Update your online inventory daily to avoid stock-outs that may occur when an Amazon buyer purchases an item from you, but you no longer have that item on hand. Making updates is especially important if the inventory you are selling on Amazon Marketplace is also for sale through other venues. (Amazon allows sellers to charge customers at the time of shipment, so that if you run out of stock you can cancel the order before the customer pays.)

- Before pricing your items, research prices for comparable products on Amazon Marketplace and make adjustments if necessary.

- If an item has been listed for more than 30 days and has not sold, check your pricing to make sure that it is competitive and make changes if necessary.

- The Vacation Settings feature may take up to 36 hours to remove your listings and another 36 hours to restore them. During this period, listings cannot be modified or deleted. Because of this, we don't suggest using this feature to remove your listings from the site. Read more about using this feature by visiting the Seller Account and Preferences help page.

For more information about listing on our site, please visit Amazon's help pages for listing items:

http://www.amazon.com/gp/help/customer/display.html?ie=UTF8&nodeId=1161236

These additional guidelines apply to Pro-Merchant subscribers:

• Break large Inventory Loader files into batches with fewer than 25,000 listings or file sizes smaller than 10 megabytes.

• It is not necessary to re-submit the same Inventory Loader file more than once; during peak times our systems can be very busy but be assured that we have received the file and it will be processed.

• After your file finishes processing, be sure to review the error log to determine why some of your listings may not have loaded.

• Check your Amazon Payments Account regularly for important updates on your sales, rather than relying exclusively on e-mail notifications. You can access Payments through your Seller Account.

• Provide high-quality customer service, which includes handling refunds and returns in a timely manner. Refund an order within 48 hours that you are unable to fill and issue refunds for returns within five business days of receipt. You'll find instructions on our Refunds & Invoices page.

• Use the A-to-Z Guarantee only as a last resort when resolving matters with buyers. Multiple guarantee claims are an indication of seller performance problems.

Contact Amazon.com

The following Web page enables you to send Amazon's seller support team an e-mail inquiry after logging into your account:

http://www.amazon.com/gp/help/contact-us/seller-support.html

These e-mail addresses reach Amazon technical personnel at various departments:

- Amazon Advantage: advantage@amazon.com
- Special Orders: sp-orders@amazon.com
- Search Inside the Book program: sitb-pdf-team@amazon.com
- Image uploads: image-fix@amazon.com
- Other questions or feedback: vendor-tools-help@amazon.com

A word about contacting Amazon. The company has been transitioning to a more automated system for seller support and technical support. Instead of direct e-mail and telephone calls, Amazon increasingly is emphasizing two main means of contact:

- **The "click-to-call" feature.** After logging into your Amazon account, you request a phone call from an Amazon representative. You can initiate the call from your Seller Account under the heading **Contacting Seller Support.**
- **A Web-based contact form.** For regular e-mail customer support and general questions about Amazon, initiate your inquiry using this Web-based contact form:

https://www.amazon.com/gp/help/contact-us/general-questions.html

Get help from other sellers

Sometimes the quickest, easiest way to get advice about selling on Amazon is to ask another seller. It's easy to network with other sellers on the several "Amazon Seller Community" boards hosted by Amazon, which are divided into several topics:

- Help for New Sellers

- Listing Management & Reports

- Order Management, Shipping, Feedback & Returns

- Third-Party Software & Services

- Seller Soapbox

- Seller Announcements (official notice from Amazon about technical problems and operational changes.)

- Seller Success (recommendations from Amazon's Marketplace team.)

For access to each message board, see:

http://www.amazonsellercommunity.com

Stay on the law's right side

If you're running a business, you need good records to prepare your tax returns competently. You must support the income, expenses, and credits you report on your return. Generally, these are the same records you use to monitor your business and prepare your financial statements.

Business records must be available in case the Internal Revenue Service demands an inspection at any time. If the IRS asks for an explanation of your tax returns, complete records will help conclude the examination quickly.

In addition to staying on the right side of the law, keeping good business records will help you manage your business more effectively through these critical tasks:

Monitoring your business's progress. Records will show whether your business is improving or faltering, where sales are coming from, and what changes in your practices might be appropriate. Good records give you a better chance of making your business succeed.

Preparing financial statements. Good records are essential for preparing accurate financial statements. These statements can aid in any necessary dealings with your bank and creditors, as well as help you make business decisions.

Identifying receipt sources. Your business will have money and goods coming in from various sources, and you'll need to keep this information separate from personal receipts and other income.

Your business's legal structure

Once you've decided to pursue Amazon sales, you'll need to decide how your business will be formally organized and how you'll meet your tax obligations. As your business grows, you should periodically revisit the question of the best form of organization for your business.

Sole proprietorship. Establishing a sole proprietorship is cheap and relatively simple. This term designates an unincorporated business that is owned by one individual, the simplest form of business organization to start and maintain. You are the sole owner and you take on all the business's liabilities and risks. You state the income and expenses of the business on your own tax return.

Any business that hasn't incorporated is automatically a sole proprietorship. So if you haven't incorporated, formed a partnership, or established a limited liability company, your business is a sole proprietorship by default.

The good news about a sole proprietorship is that you're entitled to all the profits from the business. On the other hand, you are 100 percent responsible for all debts and liabilities. So if your business is sued, your personal assets could be seized.

As a sole proprietorship, you're liable for paying income tax and self-employment tax (Social Security and Medicare taxes), and for filing quarterly estimated taxes based on your net income. Since you don't have an employer reporting your income and withholding a portion of your paycheck for taxes, you must inform the IRS about the income from your Amazon selling and make quarterly tax payments on the profits. Quarterly installments of the estimated tax, submitted with Form 1040-ES, are due April 15, June 15, September 15, and January 15 of the following calendar year. If you don't yet sell full-time and you also work at a job where your employer withholds income for taxes, you can ask your employer to increase your withholding. That way you might avoid having to mail in quarterly estimated payments on your profits.

As far as the IRS is concerned, a sole proprietorship and its owner are treated as a single entity. Business income and losses are reported with your personal tax return on Form 1040, Schedule C, "Profit or Loss From Business."

If you've never filed a Schedule C with the IRS before, you might wish to hire an accountant to assist you with the first year's return. The following year you might complete the return yourself. One helpful tool in this regard is tax-preparation software such as TurboTax or TaxCut. Unlike the IRS instruction pamphlets, these products guide you through the tax-filing process in plain English. The program can save you several hours at tax time because you don't have to decipher the arcane language of the IRS.

• **Partnership.** A partnership is the relationship between two or more persons who agree to operate a business. Each person contributes something toward the business and has a stake in its profits and losses. Partnerships must file an annual information return to report the income and deductions from operations. Instead of paying income tax, the partnership "passes through" profits or losses to the partners, and each partner includes their share of the income or loss on their tax return.

• **Corporation.** In a corporation, prospective shareholders exchange money or property for the corporation's stock. The corporation generally takes deductions similar to those of a sole proprietorship to calculate income and taxes. Corporations may also take special deductions.

• **Limited liability company.** A limited liability company (LLC) is a relatively new business structure allowed by state statute. LLCs are popular because owners have limited personal liability for the company's debts and actions, as is also the case for a corporation.

Local ordinances

Call your county government's headquarters to ask what types of permits and licenses are required for your business. Some cities, counties, and states require any business to get a business license. If you're working at home, your city or county may require a "home occupation permit" or a zoning variance, and you might have to certify that you won't have walk-in retail customers. Since your business is an online and mail-order business, this shouldn't be a problem.

If you are conducting your business under a trade name or your Amazon nickname, you should file a "fictitious name" certificate with your county or state government office so people who deal with your business can find out who the legal owner is. This is also known as a DBA name (Doing Business As) or an "assumed name."

Sales taxes. Although the Internet is a "tax-free zone" in many respects, this does not apply to state sales taxes for goods sold to customers in your state. To pay the tax, you'll need to open an account and obtain a "resale license," known as a resale number or sales tax certificate in some instances.

You don't collect state sales tax on orders shipped outside your state. Internet sales, as well as fax, telephone, and mail-order sales, shipped to another state aren't subject to sales tax unless you have an office or warehouse located there. In some states, shipping and handling fees are not subject to sales tax, but in some they are—you will need to investigate the issue for your home state. This is the way things operate today, but there's no guarantee it will stay this way.

Once you've made the decision that your Amazon business is no longer a hobby, obtain a resale certificate from your state tax office. This will relieve you of paying state sales tax on the items you buy for resale, but it will also obligate you to report and pay taxes on the sales you make to customers within your state.

A caveat: State sales tax is an evolving area you'll need to monitor. Because online sales are growing so rapidly, local governments are salivating at the prospect of collecting local sales taxes from Amazon sellers, no matter where the item is shipped. Sooner or later, it's inevitable that Amazon sellers will be regulated and taxed more than they are today.

Income taxes. Your form of business determines which income tax return form you have to file. For the vast majority of sellers without employees or a walk-in store, a sole proprietorship makes the most sense. As noted previously, the other most common forms of business are partnerships, corporations, and limited liability companies.

Many beginning sellers spend lots of time dreaming about what they'll be able to "write off" on their tax return, now that they have a business. Actually, what you're doing is paying taxes on your net profits. Your write-offs are the costs of doing business, such as buying inventory and paying for postage. What's left over is the profit, and you pay income tax on that.

As far as the IRS is concerned, your business must become profitable within three years or it will be considered a hobby, and none of the expenses will be deductible. For example, your mileage traveling to estate sales where you pick up inventory is deductible for tax purposes. But don't rely on your memory to keep track of such expenses. Keep a notebook in your car to document the mileage and expenses for your buying trips. If you're ever audited, the IRS will want to see documentation for your travel and other deducted expenses.

To figure your taxes, you'll need to keep track of every penny involving your business. Keep receipts and records, and put your expenses into categories such as "postage," "shipping supplies," "inventory," and so on.

Your bookkeeping chores can be greatly simplified with financial software such as Quicken. Most banks offer free downloads of your transactions, and once you set it up, Quicken can automatically categorize all your business expenses and eliminate most of the headaches at tax time. If you have a debit or check card linked to your account, you can use the card for nearly all your business transactions. Those records can be downloaded into Quicken right along with your banking records, making your bookkeeping that much simpler.

If you're familiar with bookkeeping and accounting principles, you might be able to do a better job with QuickBooks software, which is designed especially for small-business accounting.

Supporting documents. The law doesn't require any particular record-keeping technique, as long as you can plainly show your income and expenses. Your records must summarize your business transactions, showing your gross income, deductions, and credits. It's a good idea to have a separate checking account for your business so your personal funds are not included.

You should preserve the paper trail of any purchases, sales, and other transactions, including any invoices or receipts, sales slips, bills, deposit slips, and records of canceled checks. Keep documents that support your tax return organized and in a secure place. More detailed information is available in IRS Publication 583, "Starting a Business and Keeping Records."

Business use of your home. You may be able to deduct expenses related to the business use of parts of your home. This deduction is subject to certain requirements and doesn't include expenses such as mortgage interest and real estate taxes.

To qualify to claim expenses for business use of your home, you must use part of your home exclusively and regularly as your principal place of business or for storage. This means the area used for your business must be a room or other separate identifiable space, but you are not required to designate the space by a permanent wall or partition.

There are some exceptions to the "exclusive use" test. If you use part of your home for storage of inventory, you can claim expenses for the business use of your home without meeting the exclusive use test — but you must meet these criteria:

- Your business is selling wholesale or retail products.

- You keep the inventory in your home for use in your business.

- Your home is your business's only fixed location.

- You use the storage space on a regular basis.

- The space used for storage is a separately identifiable space suitable for storage.

To qualify under the regular use test, you must use a specific area of your home for business on a regular basis. "Incidental" or "occasional" business use is not regular use as far as the IRS is concerned.

- **Insurance.** Home-based businesses aren't usually covered under a regular homeowners or renter's insurance policy. If inventory items are stolen or damaged, it's probably not covered. If a delivery person or customer is injured at your home, you may be liable unless an "endorsement" or "rider" is added to your homeowner or renter's policy. The cost of the additional premium is usually quite low for a business without employees or a huge inventory, so it's well worth considering.

- **Bookkeeping.** For a small Amazon business, simple "cash basis" bookkeeping should suffice. The cash method entails recording income when money is received and expenses as they are paid. "Cash basis" does not necessarily mean your transactions are in cash, but refers to checks, money orders, and electronic payments as well as currency. If you're not familiar with the basics of bookkeeping, read *Small Time Operator: How to Start Your Own Business, Keep Your Books, Pay Your Taxes and Stay Out of Trouble* by Bernard Kamoroff.

Cash accounting is simpler to understand and use than the other type of bookkeeping, accrual accounting. Businesses are allowed to use cash accounting if annual sales are below $1 million.

- **Hiring employees.** The decision to begin hiring employees is a big step for any business. Although employees can enable you to expand your selling and profits, hiring will add tremendously to your paperwork and the extent to which your business is regulated by the government. Having employees means that you need to keep payroll records and withhold income, Social Security, and state taxes, as well as Medicare and worker's compensation insurance. The states and the IRS require timely payroll tax returns and strict observance of employment laws. Penalties are usually swift and severe for failure to pay payroll taxes.

An Amazon seller struggling with a busy workload might be tempted to pay cash "under the table" for help instead of actually hiring employees during their transition from a one-person shop to employer status. Don't do it. There is no gray area here—such practices are illegal because payroll taxes and worker's compensation insurance aren't being paid.

An alternative to taking on employees is to hire independent outside contractors. You can hire contractors as needed, and the practice entails less paperwork and none of the headaches of paying employment taxes or producing payroll tax returns.

If you hire an independent contractor, make certain the person doing the work understands completely that they are not an employee. Numerous small-business owners have gotten into scrapes with state and federal regulators when their independent contractors were later denied unemployment compensation or were found not to have paid their own Social Security taxes. Also, be aware that the IRS has been tightening up its rules on which types of workers can be considered independent contractors.

Consult a professional financial advisor for more information.

Stay on Amazon's good side

Amazon has a variety of policies regarding the conduct of sellers and the merchandise that can be offered on its site.

For example, Amazon has a number of policies prohibiting sellers from using a seller nickname that emphasizes what Amazon calls "external branding." In other words, Amazon doesn't want your seller nickname to be an advertisement for your own Web site.

Prohibited seller names. Seller nicknames and listings can't mention an e-mail address or a Web site URL. Here are Amazon's guidelines:

Do not divert transactions or buyers. Any attempt to circumvent the established Amazon.com sales process or to divert Amazon Marketplace participants to another Web site or sales process is prohibited. For example, sellers are prohibited from including e-mail addresses or any other reference to an external Web site in listing comments.

Advertisements. Listings that are intended wholly or mainly as "portals" to commercial or private Web sites for the purposes of advertising, or that offer contact information for non-Amazon.com transactions, are prohibited. Links to outside Web sites intended to sell items—particularly those with non-Amazon.com ordering tools or information—are prohibited. Promotional logos to credit outside services are prohibited.

These community rules are posted on this help page:

http://www.amazon.com/gp/help/customer/display.html?no deId=537780

You're violating Amazon policy if you use any of the following in your nickname or listings:

- **Domains.** Examples are com, ca, and net.

- **URL/email symbols.** For example, www, or @.

- **Names for URL/email symbols.** For example: dotcom, dtcom, atdotnet.

If you need to change your seller nickname, here is the procedure:
1. Go to your Seller Account page:

http://www.amazon.com/gp/seller-account/management/your-ac-count.html

2. Click **Edit your seller settings.**
3. Next to your nickname, click the **Edit** button.
4. Enter your new nickname, and click **Submit.**

In most cases, changes will appear live on the Web site within 24 hours.

Prohibited items

Amazon restricts the sale of these items:

- **Promotional media.** Promotional versions of all media--including books (advance reading copies and uncorrected proofs), music, and videos (screeners)--are prohibited. These items are distributed for promotional consideration and are not authorized for retail distribution or sale.

- **Unauthorized and unlicensed merchandise.** All media—including books, CDs, VHS tapes, and DVDs sold through Amazon Marketplace—must be fully licensed and authorized versions. All items sold through Amazon Marketplace must be commercially produced and authorized or licensed as a retail product.

- **Recopied media**. Copies, dubs, duplicates, or transfers of books, music, videos, television programs, radio programs, concerts, DVDs, software, etc., are prohibited. Recopied media infringe upon copyrights and trademarks and are illegal to sell. Just as you cannot sell a photocopied book without the author's permission, you cannot sell copies or duplicates of videos, music, video games, software, photos, or any copyrighted material without the permission of the copyright holder.

Listing rules

These guidelines are official Amazon policy excerpted from the company's Web site:

- **Don't deviate from the product format represented on a retail page**. When listing your item, you must do so on the page with the same item, in the same format. For example, you may not list a cassette tape of U2's *War* with an Amazon.com CD of the same recording.

- **Limit contact to transaction partners**. Amazon.com encourages buyers and sellers to communicate with one another by e-mail during an Amazon Marketplace transaction. Contact between parties must be courteous and limited to transaction details. Facilitating inappropriate or unsolicited contact is a violation of Community Rules.

- **Be honest about the condition of your item**. When listing an item, be careful to select the condition term that best represents the item you are posting to Amazon Marketplace. Furthermore, within the "Condition comments" field, please submit only information that relates to the condition of the Amazon Marketplace item you are selling.

• **Don't divert transactions or buyers**. Any attempt to circumvent the established Amazon.com sales process or to divert Amazon Marketplace participants to another Web site or sales process is prohibited. For example, sellers are prohibited from including e-mail addresses or any other reference to an external Web site in listing comments.

• **Don't include links in seller comments**. Listing comments that are wholly or mainly intended to divert buyers away from Amazon.com are prohibited. Thus, for example, Sellers are prohibited from including URLs in their listing comments.

• **Don't misuse the ratings and feedback forum**. Ratings help participants develop a reputation within the Amazon Marketplace community. The rating feature is a forum where buyers and sellers can evaluate the overall performance of a transaction partner. Participants may not post abusive or inappropriate feedback or include personal information about a transaction partner. Furthermore, any attempt to manipulate ratings of any participant is prohibited, please note that this also includes posting ratings to your own account. Since ratings cannot be altered, be careful to provide your transaction partner sufficient time to complete a sale before submitting a rating.

• **Delayed shipments or "pre-sells" are prohibited**. Items offered through Amazon Marketplace must be shipped within two business days of the close of a sale. In the event that an item you are offering will not be available for immediate delivery, alert your transaction partner and initiate any necessary refunds. It is important to maintain accurate inventory records, as instances of "stock-outs" could be reflected in your seller feedback rating.

• **Multiple sellers may not be aggregated into a single account**. In the interest of improving customer experience, every seller must be fully accountable for his or her customer-facing performance as measured by the Amazon Seller Performance Plan. Each seller must retain their own account.

If you notice that another seller is selling items in violation of Amazon's rules you can report it here:

http://www.amazon.com/gp/help/reports/contact-us

Product detail page offenses

The following rules apply to sellers who use Amazon's "create a product detail page" feature. Using this feature for any purpose other than creating accurate product details pages is prohibited.

- Create a Product Detail Page is to be used only to create pages for items that do not already exist within Amazon's catalogs, including other Amazon Web sites (Amazon.jp, Amazon.de, Amazon.co.uk, Amazon.fr, Amazon.ca, and Amazon.at).

- Using the Create a Product Detail Page feature to cross-merchandise or cross-promote a product is prohibited.

- Pages created via Create a Product Detail Page may not feature or contain products that are otherwise prohibited by Amazon.

- Use of false identifiable product information, including UPC Codes, when creating a product detail page, is not permitted.

- When creating a product detail page, sellers must provide only that information which pertains to the features of the product in general, not the condition of a particular item. Keep in mind that product detail pages may be used by other merchants to sell the same product. When listing an item for sale, sellers must use the Marketplace offer listing pipeline. Within the offer listing pipeline, sellers are provided an opportunity to note their item's condition, quantity, price, and other seller-specific details that are relevant to a specific listing.

- When creating a product detail page, sellers may not include HTML, DHTML, Java, scripts or other types of executables.

Content prohibited on detail pages

When sellers create a detail page on Amazon, it's the seller's responsibility to ensure that the listing complies with local, state, national, and international laws. If Amazon decides the content of a detail page is inappropriate, Amazon will alter the page or delete it. Here's Amazon's list of materials it explicitly prohibits:

- **Offensive material**. Includes crime-scene photos or human organs and body parts. Amazon.com reserves the right to determine the appropriateness of listings.

- **Illegal items**. Items sold on the Amazon.com Web site must adhere to all applicable laws. This includes the sale of items by individuals outside the United States. Some items that may not be sold on Amazon.com include: Cuban cigars, stock and securities, lottery tickets (including grab bags and raffles), illicit drugs, prescriptive devices and drugs, cable descramblers, lock-picking devices, smart cards, and any product which may lead to the production of an illegal item or illegal activity. Packaged food that meets all applicable federal, state, and local standards for sale to consumers is permitted.

- **Pornography**. Pornography, X-rated movies, home porn, hard-core material including magazines that depict graphic sexual acts, amateur porn, soiled undergarments, sexual aid devices, and "adult-only" novelty items that are primarily sold through adult-only novelty stores and erotic boutiques are not permitted. Prophylactics and other over-the-counter contraceptives may be listed. Furthermore, unrated erotic videos and DVDs, properly censored erotic artwork and magazines of the type you'd find at a typical bookstore are also permitted. All product images that contain nudity, graphic titles, and descriptions must be sufficiently concealed with censor strips.

- **Stolen goods**. If Amazon.com learns that an item listed on our Web site is not the property of the seller, or was obtained through illegal means, we will immediately cancel the listing in question.

- **Items that infringe upon an individual's privacy**. Amazon.com holds personal privacy in the highest regard. Therefore, items that infringe upon, or have potential to infringe upon an individual's privacy, are prohibited. Additionally, the sale of marketing lists (bulk e-mail lists, direct-mail marketing lists, etc.) is prohibited.

- **Solutions manuals**. Manuals or teacher's editions that provide answer keys to student textbook editions are prohibited.

- **Recopied media**. Copies, dubs, duplicates, or transfers of books, music, videos, software, images, etc., are prohibited. Just as you cannot sell a photocopied book without the author's permission, you cannot sell copies or duplicates of videos, music, video games, software, photos, etc. Likewise, you cannot sell transferred media--whether laserdisc to video, CD-ROM to cassette tape, or from the Internet to any digital format--unless explicitly approved by the author.

- **Promotional media**. Movies, CDs, software, books (including advance reading copies and uncorrected proofs), etc., that are produced and distributed for promotional use only are prohibited for sale through Amazon.com.

- **Video games**. Video games sold through Amazon.com must be full retail versions. Recopied and transferred video games are prohibited. Mod chips, silver disks, video game emulators, Sega bootdisks, game enhancers, unauthorized video game compilations, and accessories are also prohibited.

- **Software**. Only full retail versions of software may be sold through Amazon.com. Software that has been copied or duplicated in any format is prohibited. Additionally, academic, OEM, back-up, fulfillment, promotional, beta (prerelease), unauthorized freeware/shareware, and "softlifted" software versions are prohibited.

- **Movies**. Copies of movies (VHS, DVD, etc.) may not be sold through Amazon.com. Also, movies that have been transferred from one format to another are not permitted. For example, NTSC to Pal and Pal to NTSC conversions are not permitted. Unreleased/prereleased movies, screeners, trailers, unpublished and unauthorized film scripts (no ISBN number), electronic press kits, and unauthorized props are prohibited.

- **Television programs**. Copies of television programs, including pay-per-view events, are prohibited. Commercially produced and licensed copies of television programs are permitted. Unauthorized television programs and programs never broadcast, unauthorized scripts, unauthorized props, and screeners are prohibited.

- **Music**. Recopied music in any format is prohibited. Bootlegs, unauthorized live concerts, unauthorized soundboard recordings, unauthorized merchandise, etc., are not permitted.

- **Satellite**. Any item that enables unauthorized transmission/reception of a satellite broadcast/signal is prohibited. This includes H cards, test cards, smart cards, etc.

- **Replicas of trademarked items**. The sale of unauthorized replicas, pirated, counterfeit, and knockoff merchandise is not permitted. For instance, replicas of Rolex watches may not be posted on Amazon.com.

- **Rights of publicity**. Celebrity images and/or the use of celebrity names cannot be used for commercial purposes without permission of a celebrity or their management. This includes product endorsements and merchandise such as posters, mouse pads, clocks, clothing and unauthorized celebrity image collections.

- **Domain names**. Because of the legal complexities regarding the sale of domain names and the potential for trademark or copyright infringement, the sale of Internet domain names is prohibited.

- **Firearms, ammunition, and weapons**. Amazon.com does not permit the listing of projectile and concussive weapons that employ gunpowder or explosives. The prohibited list includes, but is not limited to, ammunition, rifles, shotguns, pistols, other firearms, and fireworks. Other prohibited items include: automatic knifes, throwing stars, spring-loaded knives, switchblades, crossbows, hunting bows, gravity-assisted knives, butterfly knives, throwing knives, nunchaku, weighted clubs, brass knuckles, BB guns, paintball guns, pellet guns, tasers , stun guns, pepper spray, mace, blowguns, weapons designed to be concealed, and any other item deemed inappropriate for the Amazon.com community. Toys that fire rubber pellets or foam darts are permitted.

- **Advertisements**. Listings that are intended wholly or mainly as "portals" to commercial or private Web sites for the purposes of advertising, or that offer contact information for non-Amazon.com transactions, are prohibited. Links to outside Web sites intended to sell items--particularly those with non-Amazon.com ordering tools or information--are prohibited. Promotional logos to credit outside services are prohibited.

- **Products that have been recalled by the Consumer Product Safety Commission (CPSC)**. The CPSC is a federal regulatory agency that is committed to ensuring that only safe consumer products are available to the public. Amazon.com wants to ensure that the products offered through our site are safe and do not pose a risk to our participants; therefore, items that have been recalled by the CPSC are prohibited. For a comprehensive list of recalled items, please visit the U.S. Consumer Product Safety Commission Web site.

- **Living creatures and unauthorized/illegal wildlife products**. The sale of live creatures and illegal wildlife products is prohibited, and this includes any type of pet or livestock. Furthermore, the sale of unauthorized wildlife items is prohibited. This includes illegal animal byproducts (skins, organs, tissue, bones, feathers, etc.) of animals and endangered species. As with all products posted to our site, please be sure to conduct proper research to ensure that your product is in compliance with all laws. The sale of plants is permitted. Also, the sale of live shellfish and crustaceans is permitted, as long as the seller adheres to all state and federal laws concerning the delivery and sales of these perishable food items.

- **Real estate.** Real estate laws and commission structures differ dramatically from state to state. Because of the legal complexities regarding the sale of real estate, real estate is not permitted for sale through our site.

- **Wine and other alcoholic beverages.** Local, state, and national government agencies heavily regulate the transaction of wine and other alcoholic beverages. Conducting sales of alcoholic beverages can be legally complex in nature; therefore, they are prohibited for sale through our site.

- **Tobacco and tobacco products.** Cigars, cigarettes, and other tobacco products are prohibited.

Software sales

Only full retail versions of software may be sold on Amazon. Software that has been copied or duplicated in any format is prohibited. Also, selling academic, OEM, backup, promotional, or beta (pre-release) software or unauthorized freeware or shareware is prohibited. Other prohibited items:

- **Duplicated software:** This is software that has been copied onto CD-R, CD-W, floppy disk, or any blank media not replicated by the original manufacturer.

• **Academic software:** This is software sold to students and faculty, and to educational institutions expressly for use by those individuals. Since Amazon.com has no way of verifying that the seller or buyer meets these requirements, the sale of this type of software is prohibited on Amazon.com.

• **OEM software:** OEM stands for Original Equipment Manufacturer. This is software that comes bundled with, installed on, or packaged with computer hardware. This software is licensed for use only with the specific hardware. Therefore, you cannot sell the software on Amazon.com unless you are also selling the hardware to the same person.

• **Promotional:** This is software distributed freely by manufacturers to promote their products.

• **Beta (pre-release):** This is software distributed for the purpose of troubleshooting, testing, and evaluation.

• **Freeware/shareware:** This is software distributed freely by the copyright owner.

Used Software. Many PC software products require first-time buyers to register their product with the manufacturer using a serial number or password upon installation. If the original owner decides to sell the software, he or she must transfer both the disc and the original serial number or password to the buyer to properly transfer the license.

Further, once the sale has been made, the seller may need to contact the respective manufacturer to transfer the registration to the buyer so that the buyer can be eligible for technical support and/or upgrade bonus offers. Finally, some products require an activation key code upon installation. These key codes are uploaded into the manufacturer's server and render it difficult to transfer the product to a third person. Keep this in mind when listing products on Amazon Marketplace.

Amazon participation agreement

If you have any doubt about the propriety of selling items on Amazon, consult the company's participation agreement:

http://www.amazon.com/gp/help/customer/display.html?ie=UTF8&nodeId=1161302

Condition guidelines

Here are Amazon's guidelines for book conditions, new and used:

- **New:** A brand-new, unread, unused copy in perfect condition.

- **Like New:** A copy with no apparent defects or signs of use. Dust cover is intact; pages are pristine. Suitable as a gift.

- **Very Good:** A read copy that remains in excellent shape. Pages are intact, and there is no underlining or highlighting. The spine is not damaged.

- **Good:** A used but clean copy. Pages are all intact, and the dust cover is intact if issued. Some signs of wear may show on the spine, and pages might have some notes or highlighting.

- **Acceptable:** A good reading copy. All pages and the cover are intact. Pages might have extensive notes or highlighting, but all text is unobscured. Dust cover may be missing.

- **Unacceptable:** Books with mold, stains, missing pages or obscured text are ineligible for selling. Promotional copies such as uncorrected proofs and advance reading copies may not be sold.

- **Collectible.** Items priced at or above a manufacturer's suggested retail price (MSRP) of $10 or more are eligible for the Collectible designation. Items priced under $10 may be listed as New or Used but aren't eligible for the collectible designation. To be designated Collectible, books should have one or more unique characteristics that increase their value for collectors, such as being a First Edition, a first printing, signed, or a scarce printing. Certain books should never be designated collectible, including ex-library books, book club printings, or remainders. You should further explain the book's condition and other characteristics in the condition comments.

Music:

- **New:** An unused, brand-new, unopened disk or tape in perfect condition.

- **Like New:** An item without apparent use, even though it may be missing its shrink-wrap. Jewel cases or tape cases should be pristine. Enclosures, liner notes or sleeves should be in perfect condition. The item is gift quality.

- **Very Good:** A used item that remains in excellent condition and plays flawlessly. May show signs of wear.

- **Good:** Plays flawlessly but has obvious signs of wear. The case may be worn but isn't damaged. Enclosures and liner notes are unmarked, in good condition. The item might be marked with the name of a previous owner.

- **Acceptable:** Plays perfectly but shows significant wear. The case may be damaged and liner notes may be marked but remain legible and complete.

- **Unacceptable:** Music items that are unplayable, scratched, rerecorded or not manufactured by the copyright owner are ineligible for selling. Items marked as promotional, such as those distributed to radio stations, are prohibited.

- **Collectible.** Items priced $10 or above the MSRP, whichever is greater, may be designated Collectible. Items priced lower are eligible only for the New or Used designation. To be considered Collectible, music items should have one or more special characteristics that increase their value for collectors. These characteristics might include, but aren't limited to: Autographed or scarce items, special pressings, limited editions, or unusual characteristics such as colored vinyl. An explanation of the special characteristics should be included in the condition comments.

For condition guidelines for items in other categories, see:

http://www.amazon.com/gp/help/customer/display.html?no deId=1161242

Kick it up a notch

Amazon has two ways for high-volume merchants to gain extra visibility and boost sales: "Featured merchant" status and the "Merchants@" program. Both can result in a logo that enhances your seller name and placement on Marketplace. Amazon hasn't publicly divulged many details about these programs, but they seem to be dominated by large, non-media sellers. In addition to the added exposure, these merchants have another important privilege: the ability to set their own shipping rates and charge customers at the time of shipment, not the time of purchase—thus preventing the need to refund customers in case of stock-outs or other fulfillment problems.

Featured Merchant Status. Amazon provides virtually no public information about how to attain featured status. The major factors appear to be a track record on Amazon of a certain length of time with a good feedback record, do a certain volume of monthly business, and display low rates of refunds and A-to-Z guarantee claims.

Merchants@ Program. If you're invited, this Amazon program, sometimes called M@, enables you to compete for Amazon's "Buy Box" right alongside Amazon itself. However, it's a "don't call us, we'll call you" situation. If you're already doing good business on Amazon, you'll be asked to join Merchants@. Or you can express your interest by completing the form here:

http://www.amazonservices.com/contactus/

Automation

Once your Amazon business grows to a certain point, it's well worth having some tools to automate the repetitive tasks, such as repricing your inventory and sending shipment-confirmation messages. If you're handling dozens or hundreds of these transactions per day, shaving a few seconds from each task can vastly improve your efficiency.

An Amazon business can start out simply, but quickly become a technical challenge as your inventory and sales volume grow. Once you have a few thousand items in your inventory—or dozens of orders flowing in daily—you'll need a system for keeping track of everything. When Customer X sends a message asking when his item was shipped, you must be able to take care of the inquiry in just a moment. Otherwise, you'll quickly become bogged down with the minutia of day-to-day operations.

For many sellers, the answer is automation, either software or an online service that helps manage the business. Fortunately, a number of innovative products and services have been introduced in the past few years that can save you a massive amount of time.

As we've seen, shaving a bit of time on repetitive tasks can have a big cumulative effect. Depending on your business, some of the products listed here could provide the same kind of benefits by automating the manual tasks you perform from your computer.

Some of these automation tools cost a lot of money, but can be worth it if they help make your business more profitable by freeing up your time to focus on what's important—finding and listing inventory.

Get efficient with fulfillment software

Once your Amazon business grows to a certain point, it's well worth having some tools to automate the repetitive tasks, such as repricing your inventory and sending shipment-confirmation messages. If you're handling dozens or hundreds of these transactions per day, shaving a few seconds from each task can vastly improve your efficiency.

If you're a computer whiz, you can probably cobble together a good system by downloading Amazon's order fulfillment report spreadsheets. But there are several third-party software products that can download your Amazon orders automatically and automate the tasks of printing of packing slips and pick lists, as well as personalized shipment e-mails. Used in conjunction with an online postage account, these programs can print shipping labels with the correct postage, and even complete the necessary customs forms for international shipments.

Listing new items for sale can also be automated. Using a barcode scanner, you can eliminate the chore of keying in ISBNs for your new items.

Automatic repricing allows you to quickly cut your price in response to competition in order to facilitate sales, and to raise your prices to pad your profits when possible. Done correctly, this price optimization can maximize your sales velocity, cash flow, and free up shelf space for new stock.

Try the evaluation versions of software when they are available, and test the responsiveness of the company's technical support. If the company isn't responsive when you make an inquiry before purchasing, you can assume they will not be of great help after they've collected your money.

You should also consider the risk of leaving the proper functioning of your business operations at the mercy of a small entrepreneurial company. Your business can be damaged severely if your vendor's system goes haywire and can't be fixed promptly. For example, what would happen to your business if Amazon suddenly redesigned its system, and as a result, you could no longer use your vendor's software to manage your inventory or print packing slips? If history is any guide, you can count on this sort of thing happening periodically, so it's prudent to have a backup plan for how you'll operate when a vendor is down.

Some vendors faced with unexpected technical challenges have simply ceased operations, leaving their clients without service or refunds. In certain cases, payments may be recovered, but the larger issue is what happens to your business if it is held hostage to a service provider or piece of software that quits working.

If you're in the market for one of these services, check the vendor's Web site for testimonials from other reputable sellers. If you don't see any testimonials, ask the company for references. Any reputable company with a good product has no problem providing a list of happy clients.

Fees can add up quickly. Some vendors charge a modest one-time licensing fee for their software, but others want a cut of your monthly sales. Consider whether this fits with your business model. If your monthly gross on Amazon is just a few hundred dollars now, a fee of 3 percent in exchange for the use of a nifty service might seem fair. But what if your business expands to the point that your monthly gross is $10,000? Will you think that $300 a month, $3,600 a year, is fair for using that software?

And before signing up with a third-party automation tool, sell on Amazon for several months without any special software at all. That way, you'll fully understand the benefits of automation whenever you decide to add it, and you'll know exactly how much it's worth to you.

Since Fulfillment by Amazon is a relatively new program, not all third-party software vendors have added support for FBA. However, Amazon has created an application programming interface, or API, for FBA enabling merchants and software developers to integrate their computer systems directly. For more information, send an e-mail to fba@amazon.com or fba-sdk-questions@amazon.com).

For a full list of third-party software providers, visit this page:

http://solutions.amazonwebservices.com/connect/kbcategory .jspa?categoryID=74

Do-it-yourself bulk listing

If you're reasonably proficient with computer spreadsheets, you can probably bulk-upload your new product listings to Amazon without buying software or paying monthly subscription fees? In any case, investigating the do-it-yourself bulk listing option will help you understand what the fee-based third-party listing tools are accomplishing for you, and whether they're worth the money.

Amazon offers a free bulk-listing tool for Pro-Merchant sellers called "Inventory Loader." If you list dozens of new products each week on Amazon, switching to the Inventory Loader (as opposed to listing manually using the "Sell Yours Here" button") can save lots of time. You'll upload your listings all at once, instead of one at a time, clicking through Amazon's listing pages.

After a bit of practice with the Inventory Loader, you can input your new listings in a matter of seconds, just by plugging in a few bits of information.

In addition to the time savings, the Inventory Loader brings two valuable side benefits: It generates backup copies of all your listings, which you can save to your PC. And using this handy data file, you can list your inventory on additional selling venues that accept bulk uploads.

To use the Inventory Loader, you'll need to use "spreadsheet" software. If you're not already familiar with spreadsheets, your computer may already have such a program preinstalled, such as Microsoft Excel or Microsoft Works, both of which allow you to manage spreadsheets. If you don't have either one of these, a free alternative is the open-source software suite called OpenOffice. You can download the OpenOffice spreadsheet and other programs here:

http://openoffice.org

Working with spreadsheets

A spreadsheet is simply a grid of information, a table. It's an easy way to manage a bunch of data, like your listings. Across the top row are the "fields" of information—columns labeled **ISBN**, **Price**, **Condition**, and so on. Each descending row contains the particulars about one of your listings. Here's a simplified example:

ISBN	Price	Expedited shipping
0743226720	12.00	Y
0446310786	5.25	N

The top horizontal row shows the data fields. The next row down is the first listing, indicating its ISBN, price, and whether expedited shipping is offered for the listing. When each blank cell of the spreadsheet contains the details of that listing, the file is uploaded to Amazon, and within minutes, all those listings will be live.

Here's how to get started with this method. Start out with a single product, just to make sure things are working correctly. Download a copy of Amazon's Inventory Loader template, which saves us the trouble of designing your spreadsheet from scratch. Navigate here:

http://s1.amazon.com/templates/MyAmazonInventory.xls

Now save this template to your hard drive: In your browser, click **File**, **Save as**, and name the file:

Template.xls

Now open your template using the spreadsheet software—Excel, Works, or OpenOffice. Click **File**, **Open**, and enter your file name, template.xls.

Entering a listing. Now populate the data fields for our first listing, from left to right:

1. **product-id.** Here you'll enter the product's ISBN, UPC, ASIN or EAN in the rectangular cell beneath the cell labeled **product-id.**

2. **product-id-type.** Enter 1 to indicate an ASIN; 2 to indicate an ISBN, 3 to indicate a UPC, or 4 to indicate an EAN.

3. **item-condition.** Instead of typing in the words to indicate "Very Good," "Acceptable," etc., you need only to type in a corresponding number, such as:

Like New = 1
Very Good = 2
Good = 3
Acceptable = 4
New = 11

4. **Price.** Just the number and two decimal places, no dollar sign. (This is a good time to eyeball competing listings. Copy the product identifier from your spreadsheet and search for it on Amazon.)

5. **SKU.** If you're not already using SKUs, we'll explain this one later. For now, just enter a place-holder, like A1.

6. **Quantity.** If you have a single item, enter "1."

7. **add-delete.** Enter "A" to add the item to your inventory. (To delete, enter "D.")

8. **will-ship-internationally.** Enter "Y" if you're offering international shipping on this listing. Otherwise, enter "N."

9. **expedited-shipping.** Same as above: enter "Y" for yes, "N" for no.

10. **item-note.** Here's where to enter your Sellers Comments, such as "scratch on top," etc.

11. **item-is-marketplace.** Enter "Y."

That's it. The next two fields will be populated with Amazon's catalog information after you upload. And the remaining fields don't apply to Marketplace listings, only auctions.

Now save your upload file on our disk as a text file: Click, File, Save As and give your spreadsheet a file name, such as **upload.txt.** There's also a pull-down menu where you can indicate the file type. Be sure to indicate "Text, tab-delimited."

Now upload the file. From your Seller Account, click **Upload multiple items.** Select the file type (tab-delimited) and the upload option **Add/Modify/Delete.**

In a moment you should receive an automated e-mail from Amazon with the status of your upload. If everything was satisfactory, the e-mail will indicate **1 items activated.**

Refine your template

Much of the data you entered for that first listing will be the same for all your listings. In the future, you can save time by pre-filling your template with default values, such as:

Product-id-type. Always number 2 for ISBNs.

Item-condition. For example, most of the items you list might be in "Like New" condition. Pre-fill this field with 2. For exceptions, just plug in the correct number.

Quantity. It's always 1, unless you've got more than one item in identical condition.

Add-delete. If you're adding new listings, it's always A for add.

Will-ship-internationally. You'll probably have a standard policy for your Amazon listings. Pre-fill with Y if you regularly offer international shipping.

Expedited-shipping. Same as above.

Item-is-marketplace. Always Y for Marketplace listings.

A word about SKUs

If you're unfamiliar with the term SKU, it's a retailing acronym for Stock Keeping Unit. For your Amazon business, it can be a series of symbols for identifying each unique item in your inventory.

You'll need to use SKUs to work with the Inventory Loader. On your spreadsheet, you can also pre-fill a column with SKUs. For example, your first two SKUs might be:

SKU
A1
A2

A word about ISBNs

Spreadsheets sometimes have trouble handling product identifiers such as ISBNs. The reason: These programs don't like numbers that begin with a zero, as many ISBNs do. Spreadsheets usually lop off the leading zero by default, which can introduce errors into your file.

Here's how to prevent your ISBNs from getting mangled: Click the top gray rectangle on your spreadsheet, the one labeled A. This will select (darken) your column labeled **product-id.** Then click **Format, Cells.** Click **Number, Text,** then **OK.** This formats the ISBN column as text instead of a number, and as a result leading zeros will remain as you intended.

For more details on the Inventory Loader and using SKUs to manage your inventory, consult this section of Amazon's site:

http://www.amazon.com/gp/help/customer/display.html?no deId=1161312

Source used items for resale

Selling used items is a great way to start on Amazon. The profit margins on used items can be extremely healthy, although finding good items takes time. To efficiently find items that can be resold profitably, you'll need sources in your area where you can regularly find a variety of items at reasonable prices. Here's where to start:

- **Library sales.** Many public libraries periodically sell used and new books, videos and audio recordings. Sometimes these items are being discarded by the library, but often they are excess donations from the public. These fund-raiser sales are organized by local "Friends of the Library" chapters. Sales schedules are posted here:

http://www.booksalefinder.com/

Many libraries also have a small daily book sale at a shelf or cart near the lobby, and some larger library systems even operate a full-time used bookstore. Sometimes these stores, tucked away in a library basement, are unadvertised gold mines.

In addition to libraries, schools and civic groups organize book sales, and these sales can include some high-quality donated stock.

- **Estate sales.** Estate sales can be a reliable source of fine, bargain-priced items. Usually advertised in newspaper ads, these sales liquidate the entire contents of a household, and can include large groups of used items, collectibles, and unused gifts.

If you attend an estate sale, plan on being the first in the door. This can mean standing in line for 45 minutes or more at a well-publicized sale, but getting first crack at the contents can be worth the wait.

Most estate sales are held on Friday or Saturday mornings. Larger sales may begin on Thursday and continue through Sunday. Remaining items are usually marked down 50 percent on the last day, so a good sale may be worth a second visit. But don't pass up good items on Friday or Saturday because you think you'll get them more cheaply on Sunday. By then, 98 percent of the cream will be skimmed. Get the good stuff while you can.

If there are more estate sales advertised on a given Saturday than you have time to attend, it's worth doing some detective work to determine which sales are likely to have the best items. The newspaper ad should have a contact number for the liquidator running the sale. Phone ahead and ask what types of merchandise are available. Don't rely on the newspaper ad, which might prominently mention "oil paintings," for example, when only a few cheap reproductions are for sale. And it never fails, the advertisement won't mention the most valuable items being sold.

If estate sales work well for you, it's worthwhile to cultivate a relationship with the estate liquidators who work in your area. Leave your business card and ask to be notified of all upcoming sales. These contacts may also be able to alert you to collections that come up for sale outside the estate liquidation process. Likewise, familiarize yourself with local funeral directors and estate attorneys, who can alert you to good opportunities.

• **Bankruptcy sales.** When businesses or shops go out of business, often their merchandise and office equipment is auctioned off. The sales are sometimes advertised in the local newspapers. Sometimes you can get word of these sales through local bankruptcy attorneys or the clerk of your county's bankruptcy court. It can take some work to learn the proper procedures for getting access to bankruptcy auctions, but it can result in big opportunities.

Sometimes the contents of storage facilities, where people store excess household items, are auctioned or sold off. Every month, a certain number of storage units must be cleared out by companies like Public Storage when the contents are left unclaimed and the owner quits paying storage fees. Sometimes these sales are advertised, but it doesn't hurt to ask local storage companies to notify you of these opportunities.

• **Garage sales** and **yard sales**. Weekend neighborhood sales can be a good source of stock if you enjoy wheeling and dealing. Garage and yard sales require lots of legwork, though, and the proportion of junk to gems can be high.

The main problem is that these sales are full of the stuff people no longer want, in contrast with an estate sale that liquidates the entire contents of a household. Some yard salers have caught on to this difference and now advertise their garage sales as "estate sales," aiming to draw more buyers. When you're scanning the classifieds, beware of yard sales masquerading as estate sales. An "estate sale" that does not advertise items like antique furniture, silver, and stemware might be a yard sale in disguise.

• **Thrift shops**. Thrift shops can be worthwhile sources of merchandise, particularly when the items are mispriced. Sometimes items are worth more online than in a physical store. Church thrift shops are a potential source of stock too. The prices are usually reasonable and the donated items are sometimes of higher quality than those at commercial thrift shops.

• **Close-out merchandise.** Local retail stores have only a certain amount of time to sell items they're carrying. At some point, the remaining items (such as winter clothing or last year's stereo equipment) are marked down for clearance, perhaps at more than 50 percent off.

In some stores, this clearance merchandise may be displayed in tables in the front of the store. If you talk to the store's manager, you can often get this clearance merchandise for even less—and you may find out about other bargains stuck in the back room.

You're in a strong bargaining position if you can offer to haul off a quantity of merchandise. If a store can't move clearance items fast enough, the retailer might have to sell it to a liquidator for 10 percent to 15 percent of retail. You can probably offer a bit more than the liquidators. For example, by getting the goods at 80 percent off retail, and reselling it on Amazon at 40 percent off retail, you're making a healthy profit.

Factory stores and outlet mall stores fall into this same general category. Their merchandise turns over rapidly, presenting a constant stream of opportunities.

One note of caution: Don't gamble on a large quantity of merchandise without researching to see how much it's selling for on Amazon. If there's no demand for the stuff, it doesn't matter if you get it for 99 percent off retail. It will still be dead money.

- **Overstock distributors.** New items that have been returned from retail stores can be a profitable source of inventory. In this case, you're buying from the liquidators that have already cleared merchandise from retailers. If you buy the right items, this can be a good sideline to your used-merchandise business, expanding your volume and profits. You can get identical items in quantity, and re-use the same photos and descriptions for subsequent listings, saving time. However, the average profit margin will be probably be lower than for used items. Be careful to avoid buying items that are already in plentiful supply on Amazon because price competition among sellers can eliminate your profits.

Live auctions

Scan your daily newspapers for notices of local auctions. You'll find news of estate auctions, bankruptcy auctions, and sometimes auctions dealing with specific types of merchandise or office equipment.

- **Postal Service auctions.** The U.S. Postal Service conducts public auctions at mail "recovery centers" around the country to liquidate unclaimed, damaged, and claim-paid merchandise. The lots vary in size, but tend to be large and heavy.

Most of the items in Postal Service auctions are like-new or brand-new items that have simply come unpackaged and separated from the delivery address in the mail. However, the auctions are potluck—sometimes there's no list of the exact contents, which can include miscellaneous items. The value of the individual items can range from practically nothing to hundreds of dollars. These auctions can present good buys, but whether it is worth your while will depend on what is included in the lot and how high the bidding goes.

For details on upcoming Postal Service auctions, check this Web page:

www.usps.com/auctions

In addition to auctions, the Postal Service occasionally conducts sales of personal property or its own equipment. These sales are conducted at local post offices and are advertised in local newspapers.

- **Treasury Department auctions.** The U.S. Customs Service regularly auctions off property it has seized for trade violations, trademark or copyright violations, smuggling, drug trafficking, money laundering, and other crimes. The auctioned property includes all sorts of items and sometimes includes large lots of consumer merchandise and even motor vehicles, airplanes and boats.

Most Customs auctions are conducted in New Jersey, Texas, California, and Arizona. It's possible to get a good buy on merchandise at these sales, but as is the case with any auction, the final price for items depends on public interest and what people are willing to pay for them. It's a good idea to go early and inspect the merchandise. Payment is due at the auction. For more information, see the Treasury Department's Web site:

www.treas.gov/auctions

• **GSA Auctions.** The U.S. government's General Services Administration runs a Web-based auction system allowing registered participants to bid on a single item or bulk lots. GSA Auctions offer federal personal property ranging from commonplace items like office equipment and furniture to more specialized items like scientific equipment, heavy machinery, aircraft, boats and other vehicles. Through the Web site, the GSA allows buyers across the country to bid on and buy any of the offered items. See:

http://www.gsa.gov/Portal/gsa/ep/contentView.do? contentId=9881&contentType=GSA_BASIC

• **Government Liquidation.** This is an online marketplace that sells U.S. government surplus and scrap material to the public. The site offers more than 500 commodity categories and thousands of surplus items are added weekly. The U.S. Defense Department sells items through Government Liquidation, which also runs the Web site Liquidation.com. See:

http://www.govliquidation.com

• **Law enforcement auctions.** Local police agencies often sell used equipment and recovered stolen property. There are many Web sites that advertise police auctions, but you can also find out about upcoming sales by simply calling your local police department. Ask if you can be put on a mail or e-mail list so you'll be notified of future sales. Check the classified section of your local newspaper for announcements and the Web sites **PoliceAuctions.com** and **PropertyRoom.com.**

- **Classified ads.** If you have trouble finding enough stock using the sources discussed above, try placing a classified advertisement yourself: "Cash paid for your used items."

If you place an ad offering to pay people cash, you'd better be ready for a response. The challenge is keeping the nuisance responses to a minimum. Don't give anyone the impression that you're itching to spend a wad of cash on any old junk. Keep expectations low. One strategy that seems to work is offering a "finder's fee" for referrals to a collection you agree to buy.

Ads in metropolitan daily newspapers are costly, so look for alternatives such as weekly newspapers and circulars like *Penny Saver* and *Thrifty Nickel.* Another option is CraigsList.com, the online classified service, which is free. The home page displays classified ads for the San Francisco Bay area, but you'll find a link to your nearest metro area.

While you're at it, don't overlook other free forms of local advertising, such as bulletin boards in local stores and community centers, and signs and posters.

- **eBay.** Many sellers get bulk lots of items being sold at a discount. Each and every day there are hundreds of bulk lots of used and new merchandise listed on this section of eBay:

http://pages.ebay.com/catindex/catwholesale.html

One way you can save money with a wholesale lot is limiting your search to sellers in your area. That way you can inspect the goods before bidding and haul the merchandise yourself, saving on shipping.

Get merchandise on consignment

If enough people know you're an online seller, eventually someone may ask you to sell some of their items. And while consignment selling produces several unique challenges, it is a surefire way of expanding your business.

Consignment selling solves the main problem for someone starting a new online business: finding enough merchandise to sell at prices low enough to bring a profit. With the consignment model, people bring the merchandise to you, and after you sell it, you pocket a commission less your expenses. If it doesn't sell, you return the item to its owner.

The potential is huge with consignment selling. Think of the millions of people who are interested in getting cash for their old possessions, but don't have the initiative to sell online themselves. Many of these folks probably realize they could get much higher prices for their items by letting someone else sell them online, rather than holding a yard sale.

Pitfalls await the consignment seller, though. To do it right, you need to set up a real bookkeeping system. You'll need good insurance coverage if you store merchandise belonging to someone else, in the event of fire, flood, or some other disaster. There's also the problem of managing the expectations of the folks you're accepting merchandise from. Popular shows such as "Antiques Roadshow" have convinced too many people that treasures are lurking in their attic or basement. Lots of the stuff isn't valuable, it's just old. You don't want to be roped into babysitting someone else's junk.

And perhaps the biggest consideration of all for potential consignment sellers: Are you a "people person?" Do you enjoy being around other people and getting input regarding your business from lots of different folks? If you are indeed a people person, you might find the business invigorating. On the other hand, if you're not, it might be a pain in the neck.

If you want to keep your business as simple and worry-free as possible, avoid consignment selling. If the items offered for consignment look good to you, offer to buy them outright. Sell them yourself and avoid the hassles of a consignment deal.

Explore Seller Central

Seller Central is a Web interface that enables sellers to manage their participation in two programs:

- **Fulfillment by Amazon.** This program allows sellers to have Amazon handle the shipping of their merchandise, and is covered in a subsequent section of this book.

- **WebStore.** Sellers use these Amazon-hosted Internet stores to sell independently from Amazon, although they accept Amazon-processed payments.

Seller Central enables merchants to manage inventory, sales taxes, shipping rates, images, and promotions, and to manage a Web site.

The URL for Seller Central is:

http://sellercentral.amazon.com

Some observers speculate that Amazon will move all its "pro" sellers to Seller Central. For the time being, only Amazon Marketplace sellers who begin using Fulfillment by Amazon are required to migrate to Seller Central. When sellers ask to migrate to Seller Central, Amazon transfers all their account data to Seller Central—their inventory, orders, feedback, and Amazon Payments details. From that point on, sellers use Seller Central to manage their business on Amazon.

After sellers migrate to Seller Central, Amazon doesn't allow them to switch back to a regular Marketplace account.

Through this interface, the administrator of a Seller Central account can grant permission to other company employees to use the site. This alleviates the need for a company owner and multiple employees to use the same login and password to access a seller account. The "Rights Manager" feature enables administrators to grant these other users access they need to do their jobs. For example, one employee might be granted access only to view and edit listings, or administrative rights for certain functions.

Some time ago, when Amazon debuted Seller Central, it was known by the name "Marketplace 2.0." At first it was referred to as the new interface required for using Fulfillment by Amazon.

Use Seller Central

Download an order report. To request an order report on Seller Central, follow these steps:

- On the Orders Report page, click New Orders in the navigation bar.

- In the Request an Order Report section, select the number of prior days you would like to include: 1,2,7,15, 30 or 60.

- Click the Request Report button.

A status box appears confirming your request and begins processing your order information to produce the report.

Customize your home page. Your Seller Central home page displays information about your account and special announcements from Amazon. You can customize the home page to view additional information:

- Widgets that track your sales and storefront performance.

- Dynamic help content targeted for the features you use.

- Important messages from Amazon.com.

To customize your page, follow these steps:

1.   On the Seller Central Home Page, click the **Customize this page** button near the bottom right corner of the page. The Customize Your Personal Seller Central Home Page window appears:

2.   Check the box next to the content you want to show on your home page, then click **Update.** To remove content, clear the check box.

3.   Return to your Seller Central home page, and your preferred content appears.

Customer communication guidelines

1.   **Shipment Confirmation e-mail.** Prompt notification of order status is a basic expectation of Amazon customers. Merchants are required to communicate with customers using a Shipment Confirmation e-mail upon shipping customer orders. The message should state the buyer address, items shipped and quantity, shipping carrier used with a tracking number, and the expected date of delivery. An easy way to ensure compliance with these requirements is to use Amazon's Shipping Confirmation e-mail Template.

2.   **Order Unavailable e-mail.** Merchants must commu-
     nicate with customers if the product ordered isn't
     available for shipment. You should adjust the full order
     amount using the **Manage Your Orders** feature in
     Seller Central, or use an adjustment feed. Merchants
     must use "NoInventory" or "CouldNotShip" as the reason
     codes for such adjustments. Use the "Order Unavailable"
     e-mail template to notify the customer about your inabil-
     ity to fulfill the order. The message must confirm that the
     order amount was adjusted and state the reason the item
     was unavailable. In cases where you expect to be able to
     fulfill the order but shipment might be delayed beyond
     the advertised delivery time, you're required to notify the
     customer about such delays. If the customer decides to
     cancel the order, you should start the refund process
     promptly.

3.   **Return confirmation e-mail.** When a customer re-
     turns an order, merchants are expected to acknowledge
     the item has been received. Use the Return Confirmation
     e-mail template for this message. The e-mail must in-
     clude confirmation of the items returned, and the
     amount and date of the refund. You must process the re-
     fund using the **Manage Your Orders** feature in Seller
     Central or with an adjustment feed.

Indirect Communication

Amazon's Web site displays relevant order-related information to
your customers through their "Your Account" updates. These updates
state whether the order has shipped (including the tracking number) or
whether the order was adjusted and refunds processed. These updates
depend on merchants submitting the following feeds:

1.   **Fulfillment/ship confirmation feed.** This feed tells
     Amazon.com that merchants shipped customer orders

and provides relevant order tracking information for customers.

2. **Adjustment feed.** This feed is the only way Amazon.com knows about processing refunds for customers. Because customers are curious about their refund status after they return items, this is an important feed merchants must transmit to Amazon after receiving returns. You can also use the **Manage Your Orders** feature in Seller Central to post a refund.

Seller Desktop

Seller Desktop is a Windows desktop software application enabling sellers to easily list products on Amazon. Using its interface, you can upload products, create variations, list offers against products already in Amazon's catalog, and import product data.

To run Seller Desktop, you'll need a Windows machine with at least:

- Windows Vista, XP, 2000 SP3, or 2003, and:

- A Pentium III processor

- 256 MB RAM

- 150 MB hard drive space

During the installation, you may be required to install these additional Microsoft components:

- Microsoft SQL Server 2005 Express

- .NET Framework 2.0

- Microsoft Web Services Enhancements

For more information about Seller Desktop and to download the program, visit:

https://sellercentral.amazon.com/gp/help/200128450

Listing new products with Seller Desktop. You can add a product not currently in Amazon's catalog by inputting the product data at the bottom of Seller Desktop's main interface. You can also create a "variation" (to designate blue or white gloves, or long-sleeve or short-sleeve) by entering the "parent" product, such as gloves or shirts, in the form at the bottom. After entering the category and product type fields, select **Parent** in the variation field drop-down menu. Select the variation theme, then click **Autocreate**. A dialog box will appear in which you may enter the "child" variations, such as blue gloves and white gloves.

Create an offer against an existing product. You can create an offer against a product already on Amazon by following these steps:

- Open the **Getting Started** Pane and select the **Add Amazon Item** command.

- From the Add menu, select **New Item** from Amazon's Catalog.

- After choosing one of the above options, select the category in which you want to search, enter a search keyword, and click the **Search** button. When you find the product you want to list an offer against, click the **Add** button to add it to your inventory and then click the **OK** button to close the window.

• Next, change any remaining data in the form interface such as product type, item type, quantity, or price, and then click the **Finish** button.

• You can view more detailed help on creating an offer against a product on Amazon by opening the Seller Desktop Help menu, then selecting **Seller Desktop Help**.

Upload products to Amazon

You can use Seller Desktop's Upload Wizard to upload products either of two ways:

• Open the **Getting Started** pane and click **Upload**.

• From the **Tools** menu, select **Upload.**

• Enter your Seller Central e-mail address and password and then click the **Next** button. When the upload is finished, click **Finish** to close the Upload Wizard. Your product data is then sent to Amazon, and the product status changes to **Processing.**

• Once Seller Desktop verifies that Amazon has received the products, their status changes to **On Amazon.**

Importing products to Seller Desktop. You can import product data into Seller Desktop using two types of files: text files or Microsoft Excel files. Seller Desktop will import Amazon text files, text files from your product database, or files from your accounts with other shopping venues, such as Google's Froogle.com or eBay's Shopping.com. To import your product data, select the **Import** command:

• Open the Getting Started pane and click the **Import Items** option.

• From the File menu, select **Import**.

- Then select the file that you want to import. When you see a pre-view screen showing the product data to be imported, click **Import.** When the import summary screen displays, click **Finish.**

Detail information on WebStore. If you're a WebStore merchant, detail information you add via Seller Desktop doesn't automatically appear on your WebStore. Detail information for each product in your WebStore must be content you have submitted to Amazon—including the image, title, features, description, and other details. If you haven't submitted content for a specific field for products in your WebStore, that content won't show up on your WebStore. More guidance is available in the WebStore FAQ:

http://webstore.amazon.com/Online-Store-FAQ/

Amazon product information

For Seller Central sellers, Amazon has so-called **Item Classification Guides** and **Browse Tree Guides**, where you put your products to maximize their exposure to shoppers who are browsing or searching Amazon. The current categories are:

- Apparel
- Automotive
- Baby Products
- Camera & Photo
- Electronics
- Gourmet Foods
- Health & Personal Care
- Home & Garden
- Home Improvement (formerly Tools & Hardware)
- Jewelry
- Musical Instruments

- Office Products*Pet Supplies
- Software
- Sporting Goods
- Toys & Games
- Video Games

Handle your fulfillment

As discussed previously, your business will run smoother and be more competitive if you manage your customer communications on a daily basis—that's the mental part of customer service. Now we'll turn our attention toward the physical job of handling orders.

Standardizing the way you handle customer orders will minimize mistakes and help you operate faster and more efficiently. Devising a routine way of storing, retrieving, and packing items for shipping can help you save a bit of time with each transaction, leading to huge cumulative time savings. And, as they say, time is money.

Likewise, striving to obtain the best rates on postage and delivery confirmation has a huge cumulative effect on your profitability.

Ship efficiently

Determine which type of shipping containers and other materials you'll need to ship your items, and be sure to keep adequate packing supplies on hand. The less time you spend each day scrounging around for the proper packing materials, the more time you'll have for finding and listing new merchandise.

Three popular choices for packaging smaller items are cardboard boxes, corrugated boxes and bubble mailers. The type and value of the item being shipped can call for different materials. Padded or bubble envelopes may be fine for small, inexpensive items, but for more fragile and valuable items, use a box to protect them from bending and crushing.

If you've reached the point where you're shipping more than two packages a day, it's time to consider using an online postage service.

Monthly service fees are $15 or less, allowing you to avoid standing in line at the Post Office. Instead, you'll be able to prepare your shipments at your PC and drop off crates of parcels at your Post Office's rear dock. You also can submit a request for "Carrier Pickup," and a Postal Service truck driver will pick up your packages at your house for no charge.

Another advantage of using online postage is that it can simplify your record-keeping by automatically compiling a file of your shipments and tracking numbers. Records on each parcel shipped can be retrieved instantly—no rummaging through paper receipts. Online postage also enables you to purchase insurance coverage, signature-confirmation service, and other add-ons without having to wait in line at the Post Office.

Another draw of Internet postage services is the option to print "stealth" postage, which hides the value of the postage fees you paid on each package. Instead, the label merely indicates the weight of the package, and the statement "U.S. Postage and Fees Paid." This reduces customer complaints that the shipping fee they paid exceeded the postage cost.

Each of the several online postage services offers different features and the services charges vary:

- **Endicia.com.** Endicia enables users to print U.S. postage on an envelope, label, or piece of paper from a laser printer or a dedicated thermal label printer. Endicia is easy for beginners to use but also has advanced capabilities for high-speed batch printing when needed.

  Customer addresses can be imported from a database or copied from the clipboard. Users get free delivery confirmation on Priority Mail parcels. For Media Mail parcels, users get a discounted "electronic rate" for delivery confirmation compared with the "retail" fee when paying at the Post Office.

  Endicia also enables users to purchase insurance from U-Pic Insurance Services, which offers more competitive rates than the Postal Service.

  Fees. Users pay $9.95 monthly or $99.95 annually for the basic plan, and $15.95 monthly or $174.95 annually for premium service. A

30-day free trial is available. The premium service includes more automation capabilities and the ability to print stealth postage.

- **Stamps.com.** Stamps.com's online postage service is similar to Endicia's. While it may appear simpler to learn and use, it offers fewer features and is less adaptable. Users can print stealth postage. *Fees.* Users pay $15.99 monthly.

- **Click-N-Ship.** The U.S. Postal Service enables online users to print shipping labels at this site. Registration is required for postage and batch label orders. At this time, postage may be printed only for Express Mail and Priority Mail labels. For more information, see:

https://sss-web.usps.com/cns

- **Shipstream Manager.** Shipstream is offered by Pitney Bowes, which used to be a popular source from which to rent postage meters. The recently introduced Shipstream is its first Internet postage product that has the range of features required for businesses shipping parcels.
Fees. Users pay $18.99 monthly. For more information, see:

http://www.pitneyworks.com/shipstream

- **USPS Shipping Assistant.** This free PC-based software distributed by the U.S. Postal Service creates shipping labels with delivery confirmation, signature confirmation, or Express Mail service. Users can receive discounted rates for Delivery Confirmation and Signature confirmation, and can calculate rates and send customers e-mail notification that the package is on the way, including the delivery confirmation number. Users must pay for postage separately.

For more information, see:

http://www.usps.com/shippingassistant

Other shipping resources

The Postal Service, UPS, and other carriers maintain several online resources that can help assess shipping options.

- **Domestic Rate Calculators.**
  USPS: **www.usps.com/tools/calculatepostage**
  UPS: **www.ups.com/using/services/rave/rate.html**

- **International Rate Calculators.**
  International shippers may wish to consult these resources:
  USPS: **http://ircalc.usps.gov/**
  UPS: **www.ups.com/using/services/rave/rate.html**
  DHL: **www.dhl-usa.com/shipping/**
  FedEx: **www.fedex.com/us/international**

Thermal label printers. Another big time-saver is a thermal label printer, which quickly prints 4 x 6-inch address labels like the ones used on UPS packages. Instead of constantly having to feed sheets of labels into a laser printer, you can load a dedicated thermal printer with a roll of 300 labels and it's always ready. Although these printers can cost more than $300 when brand new, used and reconditioned thermal printers are usually available on eBay for about $40. A popular model is the Zebra 2844.

Likewise, a postal scale with at least a 10-pound capacity can be a valuable time-saver. Don't risk your shipments by using a bathroom scale to weigh your packages. You don't want to apply too little or too much postage. Some of the newer electronic scales integrate with online postage services, saving you even more time because you don't need to key in the package's weight.

Choose a shipping company

Several options are available for shipping Amazon items. Among the most popular:

- **U.S. Postal Service.** If you're selling typical merchandise, the good old Post Office should be your first consideration. Although USPS takes a fair amount of criticism, its service is relatively reliable and economical. For items weighing a few pounds or less, USPS is usually the cheapest way to ship. The Postal Service also provides free shipping envelopes and boxes for users of its Priority Mail and Express Mail services. Special low rates for sellers of media such as books, music and videos make the Postal Service indispensable. Although USPS offers delivery confirmation with online tracking numbers, the system is not as reliable as those offered by competitors. For more information, see www.usps.gov.

- **United Parcel Service.** UPS is a good option for packages that are larger and heavier than the maximum accepted by the Postal Service. UPS accepts packages weighing up to 150 pounds, while the USPS maximum is 70 pounds. Nowadays many office supply stores such as Staples have UPS drop-off counters. For more information, see **www.ups.com**.

- **Federal Express.** FedEx made its name by offering overnight delivery for urgent packages. Since then the company has expanded into Ground Home Delivery service that is fairly economical and comparable to regular UPS service. For more information, see **www.fedex.com**.

Shipping materials

It's essential to have a ready supply of all the shipping containers you'll need for any item in your stock. When orders roll in, you can't afford to spend time scrounging around for a suitable box.

One reliable vendor for shipping supplies is Associated Bag Co. They offer competitive pricing and deliver by the next business day at regular UPS ground rates. Another standby is Uline, which has a larger selection of items but can be a bit more expensive. Also, Uline's shipping fees are higher, and next-day delivery costs extra. However, if you place an order for a large quantity, Uline will provide a discount and in some cases free delivery.

Cardboard bookfolds are a popular shipping container for books, but taping up each package by hand is time-consuming. As your selling volume grows, it helps to find some time-saving packing techniques, and bubble mailers can be a good option for mailing inexpensive books. Another advantage of using bubble mailers is their light weight, enabling you to ship via First Class mail for about the same cost as Media Mail. Your customers will appreciate the faster delivery time.

A disadvantage with inexpensive paper-covered bubble mailers is they are prone to ripping. Also, look for mailers with a self-adhesive strip. Cheaper mailers sometimes have no adhesive strip, so you're right back where you started with having to hand-tape each package. Jiffy Tuffgard mailers, which are made of vinyl, are perhaps the most durable bubble mailer, but are more expensive than manila-covered mailers.

Sizes 1, 2 and 4 bubble mailers will hold most standard-sized books. With cardboard bookfolds, the "digest" size holds standard-sized books, and you can get larger ones that will even hold a coffee table book. However, for expensive books, when you can't take the chance of a corner getting bumped, you'll want crushproof document mailers, which can absorb about 200 lbs of pressure.

Many smaller shipping-supply vendors can be found on the Internet with lower prices, but avoid placing a large order with a new vendor. Let them earn your confidence first.

Another option is searching for local shipping suppliers by consulting your Yellow Pages. If you can avoid shipping fees, that could add up to significant savings over time. Let them know you'll be buying often and in quantity, so they'll quote their best prices.

Shipping timeframes

Here are the shipping guidelines set by Amazon. When customers buy from you, these are shipping timeframes Amazon indicates in the checkout cart and confirmation e-mails:

- **Domestic Standard:** Should be received by your buyer within 4-14 business days (up to 21 days in some cases).

- **Domestic Expedited:** Should be received by your buyer within 2-6 business days.

- **International shipments:** Amazon specifies that international orders should arrive within 3-6 weeks after the order date, though it may take orders up to 8-12 weeks to arrive depending on customs delays. As a practical matter, though, many international customers become impatient after a few weeks because they haven't read the fine print about shipping times. So unless you can afford to ship your items via air delivery, you can expect many complaints from overseas customers. For this reason, many sellers choose not to offer international shipping for their heavy or oversized items where air shipping costs would reduce profits unacceptably.

Best practices

Amazon prescribes these "best practices" for Marketplace merchant fulfillment:

- Always ship your items within two business days of order notification. This is required.

- Include a packing slip with your item. You can print it from your Seller Account or create your own. Don't forget to include your return address. Please also review our shipping and packing guidelines carefully.

- Include a note with your package with your contact information and encourage your buyer to leave you feedback at www.amazon.com/feedback. This can be accomplished easily with a preformatted packing slip you can print through your Seller Account.

- Send buyers a ship confirmation message after you have shipped their order, and include tracking or delivery confirmation numbers if they are available.

These additional guidelines apply to Pro-Merchant subscribers:

- Pro Merchant Sellers can schedule Order Fulfillment Reports to run on a regular basis. We recommend that you schedule these reports no more than once per day. The reports generated by this URL contain data for the most recent 24-hour period.

- You can manually generate a report for 15, 30, or 60 days via your Seller Account if needed.

Q&A: Is Delivery Confirmation worth it?

QUESTION: I'm fairly new to selling on Amazon. When I sold on eBay I shipped using UPS. Now I'm using the Postal Service more because I'm selling media items.

My problem is with the Postal Service's Delivery Confirmation service. I've had several cases where the customer says they never received the item, but the Post Office shows it was scanned "delivered." I've tried the reasonable approach of filing a "lost package" report with USPS, while suggesting that the customer either wait longer or ask Amazon for an A-to-Z Refund. I close each message with a request that the customer contact me with any questions or concerns. Usually, the customer never replies, then posts negative feedback.

My complaint is with the Post Office; their service is terrible. They make a mistake by stating that a delivery was made, and stand by it no matter what. My experience with United Parcel Service has been completely different. UPS' tracking system works better, and they always refund me for lost or damaged packages. Unfortunately, UPS is too expensive to use for small media items, so I'm stuck with the Post Office.

If I'm going to end up giving a refund anyway, what's the point of Delivery Confirmation? I'm considering dropping it completely.

ANSWER: You're right, at first glance it doesn't make a lot of business sense to use Delivery Confirmation. For example, last year I tallied how much I'd spent on DC—it totaled about $4,000 for my 29,000 packages, and that was with the online discount. I don't think I got my money's worth. During that year I had less than 10 A-to-Z claims and lost packages, costing a total of less than $200.

Also, during the year I was forced to spend many hours replying to e-mails from customers who were wondering whether their package had shipped yet, even though they had received a shipment-confirmation e-mail from me. The reason is that the Postal Service rarely scans packages for the first few days after shipment. As a result, when customers check their DC number at the Postal Service's Web site, they receive a vague message like this:

> *The U.S. Postal Service was electronically notified by the shipper on February 19, 2008 to expect your package for mailing. This does not indicate receipt by the USPS or the actual mailing date. Delivery status information will be provided if / when available. Information, if available, is updated every evening. Please check again later.*

So customers who bother checking their DC number during the first few days after shipment are left scratching their head—and sometimes, they take the USPS message to mean that the package hasn't been mailed yet. So recently I decided to stop giving the DC number in my shipping confirmation e-mail. I decided it was causing more work for me, not less. It's irritating to pay good money for a service that ends up causing a bunch of extra work for you.

Why am I still using DC? One thing that is hard to quantify: How many customers who might otherwise try pulling a scam and claiming nondelivery are deterred because by the DC barcode?

Remember, Delivery Confirmation sometimes shows "delivered" even when the buyer doesn't receive the package. After all, it's not too difficult for a thief to swipe a small package from a mailbox or doorstep. As long as the mail carrier scans the package, the tracking result is "delivered," whether the buyer receives it or not. Same thing if the postal carrier drops the package at the wrong address—unless that recipient returns the package to the USPS.

Of course Amazon strongly recommends that you use DC or a tracking service. However, DC won't necessarily protect you against a nondelivery claim if the customer files an A-to-Z claim. Even when DC shows "delivered," Amazon reserves the right to debit your account for the amount of the transaction. Amazon's stated policy is that "if no receipt [by the buyer] is confirmed, the seller may still be held liable for lack of fulfillment—Amazon will not cover service errors, including loss, theft, or postal/shipping issues."

However, I'll add a few words in defense of the Postal Service, despite the aggravation they cause me. USPS Media Mail is very economical and it's the only real choice for sellers of media items working with small profit margins. And, if you're a high-volume USPS shipper, there is a way to ensure your DC numbers are scanned at the time of shipment. For example, the online postage service Endicia.com has a feature called "Bulk Acceptance Scans." It creates a single barcoded form linked to your entire day's batch of mail, which the USPS scans upon accepting your packages. So, instead of your buyer receiving a message that USPS was "electronically notified" of the package, your buyer sees that "The USPS accepted this item at [Date/Time]." To take advantage of this feature, you'll need to have a "Professional" or "Platinum" Endicia account. Other postage services also have the ability to offer this feature, which the USPS calls "Shipment Confirmation Acceptance Notice."

Excerpted from Steve Weber's "Selling Books" blog.

Outsource your fulfillment

A relatively new service, **Fulfillment by Amazon**, enables sellers to outsource all their customer-service chores to Amazon. Participating sellers can ship part or all of their inventory to one of several warehouses. Several of these Amazon Fulfillment Centers are scattered across the U.S.

With FBA, Amazon takes care of your selling, shipping and customer service, including returns support. Although it appeals mostly to high-volume sellers who might sell hundreds or thousands of items per day, Amazon is also marketing FBA to casual, part-time sellers who sell just a few items per month.

Amazon charges FBA sellers a variety of miscellaneous fees for warehousing and shipping your items, in addition to the regular Marketplace commission you'd pay if you were fulfilling the sale yourself. The fees include:

1. Per-fulfillment Order Fee (non-media items only)
2. Pick & Pack Fee
3. Weight Handling Fee

FBA is also available for merchandise sold outside Amazon's site. In other words, you could list items for sale on eBay or your own Web site, and have those orders handled via FBA. You wouldn't necessarily have to offer the merchandise for sale on Amazon.com.

It seems that small, part-time sellers see few advantages with FBA because many of them store their merchandise at home and consider their storage costs "free." However, some larger sellers, especially those where commercial warehousing space is expensive, believe the FBA storage rates are attractive.

Some sellers report brisk sales and good profits with FBA. One advocate is Randy Smythe, who sells used CDs and other media items. A few years ago, Smythe sold his wares on eBay, and his business required several full-time employees to handle shipping and customer service. But today Smythe runs a similar business on Amazon with no employees, using FBA to handle shipping and customer service. His net profits and gross profits are better with FBA than with his eBay business, Smythe says.

At one point, Smythe's eBay business, Glacier Bay DVD, was eBay's highest-volume business. The operation required six full-time employees, four part-timers, and the monthly warehouse rent was $4,500. Today Smythe runs his Amazon business out of his home with no employees, using the name inetmediasource. Thanks to FBA, he doesn't need to worry about customer service, e-mails, returns, or refunds—it's all handled by Amazon.

Here's how Smythe's business works:

- In local advertisements, Smythe offers to buy used CDs and videos in bulk from consumers.

- After acquiring the goods, Smythe inspects and cleans the items, labels them for FBA, and ships the items in cardboard boxes to Amazon's Reno, Nev., warehouse. Amazon provides United Parcel Service shipping labels, giving him a discount off regular shipping rates. The UPS driver picks up the boxes at Smythe's house.

- A few days after Amazon receives the boxes, the inventory is listed on Amazon.com and available for purchase.

Get a leg up on competition

Outsourcing your day-to-day chores isn't the only advantage to FBA. For example, Smythe has recorded a higher rate of sell-through—and faster sales velocity—since joining FBA. The reason is that FBA exposes his merchandise to buyers who normally don't purchase from third-party merchants on Marketplace, such as:

- Buyers who make it a habit to only buy from Amazon directly, and avoid purchasing from third-party sellers. (Customers might behave this way for any number of reasons—perhaps they don't trust third parties to handle the order with the same precision and speed as Amazon, or they've had a poor experience buying from an individual seller in the past. Perhaps the item is a gift, and the buyer doesn't want to take a chance on outside fulfillment or whether the item is truly "new." Sometimes the buyer wants the item gift-wrapped by Amazon.) Even when Marketplace sellers offer a substantially lower price compared with Amazon, a substantial portion of buyers still decide to buy items that are fulfilled by Amazon.

- Price-sensitive customers who want to take advantage of Amazon free shipping offers. These buyers want to use Amazon's "Super Saver" free shipping deal on orders over $25, while others are members of "Amazon Prime," which entitles them to free two-day shipping and other perks.

Both groups of buyers can get free shipping on your item. Non-FBA listings don't qualify for these free shipping deals.

So FBA's connection to Amazon's free shipping deals can boost your sales substantially. According to sellers, about 54 percent of FBA orders are shipped to customers using Super Saver shipping, and another 25 percent use Amazon Prime discount shipping. About 8 percent of U.S. marketplace sales go to overseas customers. That means only about 13 percent of U.S. Marketplace buyers pay the full freight on shipping.

Typical costs of Fulfillment by Amazon

Amazon has a variety of miscellaneous fees that apply to each FBA transaction. Certainly they are subject to change. But Smythe, whose typical FBA transaction is a CD sold for less than $25, breaks it down this way: Amazon charges him a "pick and pack" fee of 50 cents and a "weight" fee of about 7 cents. So, Randy's total FBA fee for shipping a CD is 57 cents. By contrast, when he ran his online store at eBay, his cost per shipment was about $1.56—including packaging, labor, postage, and USPS delivery confirmation.

Stargate (Ultimate Edition) (1994)

Starring: Kurt Russell, James Spader Director: Roland Emmerich
Rating PG-13

< Return to product information

Price at a Glance

List Price: ~~$9.98~~
Used: from $2.58
New: from $3.95
Collectible: from $14.50

Have one to sell? Sell yours here

| All | New (54 from $3.95) | Used (70 from $2.58) | Collectible (1 from $14.50) |

Show ⦿ All ○ ✓*Prime* offers only   Sorted by Price + Shipping ▾

Always pay through Amazon.com's Shopping Cart or 1-Click. Learn more about Safe Online Shopping and our safe buying guarantee.

All (1 to 25 of 125 offers sorted by : Price + Shipping)

Price + Shipping	Condition	Seller Information	Ready to buy?
$5.47 and eligible for Amazon*Prime*™	Used - Very Good	**Seller:** INETMEDIASOURCE FULFILLMENT BY AMAZON **Rating:** ★★★★★ **97% positive** over the past 12 months (261 ratings.) 268 lifetime ratings. **Shipping:** In Stock. • $3.99 Overnight Shipping: Get it Friday, February 29. • Free Two-day Shipping: Get it Monday, March 3. • Order within 2hr 43min for these delivery dates. International shipping available. See shipping rates. See return policy. **Comments:** Disc and artwork are in very good condition. We guarantee everything we sell!	Add to Cart or Turn on 1-Click to use your Amazon Prime benefits.
$2.58 + $2.98 shipping ⦿ LOW ITEM PRICE	Used - Very Good	**Seller:** TGOTOMJOAD **Rating:** ★★★★★ **97% positive** over the past 12 months (1387 ratings.) 1962 lifetime ratings. **Shipping:** In Stock. Ships from IL, United States Expedited shipping available International shipping available See shipping rates **Comments:** Disc, case and inserts are all in near MINT condition!!!	Add to Cart or Sign in to turn on 1-Click ordering.
$2.59 + $2.98 shipping	Used - Very Good	**Seller:** PIECEOFMINDBOOKS **Rating:** ★★★★★ **96% positive** over the past 12 months (109656 ratings.) 132031 lifetime ratings. **Shipping:** In Stock. Ships from MA, United States Expedited shipping available International shipping available See shipping rates **Comments:** Tested to play. Case wear, possible slight scratches and or missing artwork. 100% Satisfaction. Contact our prompt customer... (» more)	Add to Cart or Sign in to turn on 1-Click ordering.

FBA items get enhanced exposure on Amazon's offer listing page. The stated prices of FBA listings don't include shipping and handling, so these listings can appear at the "low-price" position on top, even though the seller's price might exceed the price of standard Marketplace listings, where the buyer must pay extra for shipping.

Like other FBA sellers, Smythe pays monthly FBA storage fees. But since CDs are so compact—and he sells 70 percent of his merchandise within a month after its arrival at Amazon's warehouse—he pays just a few dollars a month for storage. The average disk costs just 2 cents a month to store at Amazon's fulfillment center.

Certainly, Smythe's operation is close to a best-case scenario for using FBA: a business with compact, lightweight merchandise that turns over rapidly. A seller with different merchandise might be unable to make profits using FBA. Of course if your merchandise is bulkier and heavier—such as books, toys, or vacuum cleaners—FBA fees would be much higher.

Amazon charges a fee, by the cubic foot, for each SKU you have at the warehouse. Each day, Amazon calculates a cubic-foot usage, and you are assessed that fee. In general, one way to look at FBA is that it adds another 5 percent or 10 percent to your Amazon fees, in addition to the regular Marketplace commission (15 percent on media items). If FBA adds significantly to your sales volume, you might consider its extra costs worthwhile. In fact, some FBA sellers report that the program saves enough money on postage, insurance and refunds for lost packages to cover the costs of FBA.

There are some alternatives to FBA, such as Shipwire.com, which handles orders that customers place on your Web site. But the big draw of FBA is that your goods are offered directly to Amazon's 90 million registered buyers. It's a lot tougher to make sales on your own Web site, especially if you don't have much traffic, a famous name, or a long track record of customer service.

For complete information about FBA and its fees, consult this section of Amazon's Web site:

http://fba.amazon.com

Another contact method is the e-mail address **fba@amazon.com.** And another valuable source of current information is the Amazon-hosted FBA sellers' message board:

http://www.amazonsellercommunity.com/forums/forum.jspa ?forumID=29&start=0

Use FBA 'Basic Fulfillment'

"Basic Fulfillment" is Amazon's name for the FBA option in which orders are shipped to non-Amazon buyers. These purchases might originate from buyers visiting your Web site or an eBay store. With Basic Fulfillment, Amazon passes the shipping cost to you, and the cost varies depending on the type of merchandise and shipping method. You may offer three shipping speeds: standard delivery (5-7 days), two-day delivery, or next-day delivery.

In addition to the "shipping method" fee for Basic Fulfillment orders, Amazon tacks on the "pick and pack" and "weight" fees assessed on regular FBA orders. To give another example from Randy Smythe's operation: His "pick and pack" fee is 60 cents on media orders, the default shipping method fee (for "standard" shipping) is $1.90, and the weight fee is about 8 cents. So the total FBA fee for his non-Amazon customers is $2.58. It's clearly more expensive than fulfilling orders to Amazon buyers, so you'll need to examine how these costs would affect your profitability.

Basic Fulfillment orders can be initiated in two ways:

- You, the seller, can submit an "order fulfillment request" to Amazon using a Web form or an uploaded file. In this case, you'd supply the buyer's shipping address and other instructions.

- Your customers can initiate the order through your Web site if the site supports FBA's system, which uses XML, a general-purpose Web formatting language.

Competing with FBA

Using FBA provides some important advantages to sellers. Buyers who are hesitant to purchase from a third party are more likely to purchase when they know the FBA order is being handled by Amazon directly, using the same pick, pack and ship system. And there are other key advantages:

- FBA items are highlighted on Amazon's product pages with a logo emphasizing "Fulfilled by Amazon."

- FBA items are eligible for Amazon's free shipping deals—Super Saver Shipping and Prime shipping. That way, buyers can combine their Amazon and FBA items in the same shipment. Buyers can also choose one-day shipping.

- Listings can appear at the top of offer pages, in the "buy box" right along with Amazon's listing (non-media products only).

- Buyers can return FBA purchases directly to Amazon.

- You can take advantage of special promotions and variations.

- You can include your logo with the product description and on the offer listing page for non-media items.

FBA merchants can also qualify for "featured" merchant status in certain categories, providing even more visibility for your listings. Amazon doesn't disclose what criteria merchants must meet to obtain featured status, but apparently the program is linked to high sales volume, high feedback scores, and low refund rates.

You can get more information about FBA and enroll in the program by completing the Web form at this page:

http://www.amazonservices.com/fulfillment

After you accept the FBA agreement, you tell Amazon which products you want them to fulfill. You label your products and packages for shipping via UPS to an Amazon fulfillment center.

If you aren't a user of Amazon's Seller Central interface, you'll be required to upgrade to Seller Central to begin using FBA. After you confirm the upgrade, all your listings and account information will move to Seller Central. For most sellers, the upgrade takes just a few minutes, and Amazon sends an e-mail when the processing is completed. The upgrade may take longer if you have more than 10,000 listings.

FBA is one solution for non-U.S. sellers who want access to the American market. For example, sellers in Canada or elsewhere can ship their items to one of the U.S. fulfillment centers and let Amazon handle their U.S. distribution. To participate, the seller must have an Amazon.com seller account, which requires a U.S. bank account. Amazon has also launched FBA in the United Kingdom and Germany, which is used by sellers looking to expand their sales in Europe.

Drawbacks of Fulfillment by Amazon

Although FBA offers many advantages, you should consider the drawbacks. Among the most critical:

- **You'll incur monthly storage fees for all items that don't sell.** If you decide to remove the items from FBA, Amazon will charge you fees for returning them or removing and disposing of the items.

- **Items are outside your immediate control.** If a potential buyer has a question about a certain aspect of an item, you might not be able to provide an answer since you can't pull the item from your shelf to inspect it.

- **Loss of control over fulfillment.** If Amazon fumbles your order, your reputation can suffer. If you receive a negative feedback rating from a customer due to a delivery problem caused by Amazon, Amazon won't remove the negative rating.

If you are a media seller who lists the same unique items on multiple marketplaces in addition to Amazon, FBA might restrict your business. (One possible countermeasure would be segmenting your inventory. You'd have Amazon fulfill your orders from Amazon.com, while you list and fulfill different inventory items on eBay, Half.com, and other marketplaces.)

Lost or damaged FBA items

When items are lost or damaged at Amazon's warehouse and the company assumes responsibility, Amazon pays you either:

- The replacement value you specify, or

- At Amazon's option, an "applicable replacement value" specified in the FBA Replacement Value Schedule. You can't specify a replacement value greater than the lowest selling price for which you list that item for sale—on Amazon or through other venues.

Fulfillment by Amazon facts

- Sellers own and control their FBA inventory, and can have items returned at any time, although a shipping fee applies.

- There are no minimum or maximum inventory or order requirements.

- Storage fees are calculated daily for inventory the seller has in the Amazon fulfillment center on a square-foot basis.

- You can list part or all of your inventory with FBA. For products you don't register for FBA, you continue receiving orders through Amazon's Web site, and handling them as normal.

- Inventory at Amazon's site is insured against loss or damage.

- Orders are processed immediately and are packed and shipped to arrive on time by whatever method the customer selects.

- Amazon might store your inventory at one of several fulfillment centers, depending on the size and category of your merchandise, your location, and other factors. The centers have 24-hour security staffs, and your items are stowed in high-value cage storage.

- The maximum weight for an FBA item is 150 pounds. The minimum weight is 1 ounce, with Amazon rounding up to the nearest ounce or sixteenth of a pound.

- Basic Fulfillment orders are shipped in regular Amazon boxes with the usual logos and inserts. There's no option yet to use plain boxes or custom packaging.

- For Basic Fulfillment, all returns and customer service are handled by the merchant. Amazon will provide tracking numbers for the shipment and direct buyers back to the merchant if necessary.

- Basic Fulfillment orders are supposed to arrive two days after the customer places the order.

- Media items aren't assessed a Per-fulfillment Order Fee. Items qualifying as "media" include music, videos, DVDs, books, software, computer games, and VHS video games.

Best practices

Amazon provides the following guidance for FBA, although more details are available in the Fulfillment by Amazon Merchant Manual, which you can download after enrolling in the program:

Maximizing pricing on FBA: Amazon's offer listing page displays the lowest-priced items sorted at the top. Amazon Marketplace buyers usually look for the best deal possible, yet many buyers select from only the first few offers appearing at the top of the page. Sellers who combine competitive pricing and positioning on the offer page—along with an outstanding feedback rating—are in a much better position to attract buyers.

Below are some examples of how sellers can maximize unit sales and revenue using FBA on a 1-pound book. Although the book is priced higher than merchant-fulfilled (non-FBA) listings, it appears higher on the offer listing page and is eligible for Amazon's free shipping offers, Super Saver and Prime.

Example 1: One-pound book fulfilled by merchant

To get a high position on the offer listing page, the merchant is forced to lower the price:

Price	+ $10.00
Fulfillment credit	+ $3.99
Total price	$13.99
Amazon commission (15%)	- $1.50
Variable closing fee (VCF)	- $1.35
Shipping*	- $1.80
Total Revenue	**$9.34**

The buyer pays a total of $13.99, including shipping. The merchant receives $9.34 revenue after commission, fees and shipping.

*Estimated cost of Postal Service Media Mail shipping and packing materials.

Example 2: One-pound book fulfilled by Amazon

Since the offer doesn't include a shipping fee, the merchant can charge more for the book and successfully compete for the top spot on the offer listing page:

Price	+ $13.75
Fulfillment credit	+ 0.00
Total Price	$13.75
Amazon commission (15%)	- $2.06
Variable closing fee (VCF)	- $1.35
Fulfillment fee	- $0.90
Total Revenue	**$9.44**

The item is eligible for Amazon's free shipping offers, so the buyer can pay $13.75 (24 cents less than Example 1. However, the merchant gets $9.44 of revenue, 10 cents more than Example 1.

Smart FBA shipping

Accurate shipping to Amazon's fulfillment center will ensure that your merchandise is made available without delay. Here is Amazon's list of dos and don'ts to illustrate the most common errors sellers make when preparing shipments:

DOs	DON'Ts
✓ Verify that the quantity you are shipping for each SKU is equal to the quantity that you entered online for your shipment.	⊘ Do not ship items without labels unless you have received confirmation that your account has been set up for Stickerless, Commingled Inventory.
✓ Print your labels on the appropriate size paper (items: 1" x 2 5/8"; Package: 3-1/3" x 4") using a laser printer to ensure a quality image that will not blur or smudge.	⊘ Do not print product or package labels using an inkjet printer.
✓ Affix a label to each individual item using the PDF file provided by Amazon (Does not apply to approved Stickerless, Commingled Inventory accounts—see DON'Ts).	⊘ Do not affix package labels to seams where the label can be ripped, cut or distorted making it unscannable.
✓ Make sure the labels you affix to the items match the title and condition of each item.	⊘ Do not include unauthorized marketing materials with your packages.
✓ Label each container that you ship your items in placing the label next to the carrier's label.	⊘ Do not ship packages greater than 50 pounds without proper warning labels.
✓ Use a carrier that can provide a tracking number, so Amazon can track the progress	⊘ Do not combine items from different shipments in the same package. Item quantities must match shipment quantities in the Shipping Queue.
✓ Enter tracking numbers into the Shipping Queue using the "Ship and Track" button.	⊘ Do not ship more items than the quantity you entered online for the Shipment.
	⊘ Do not leave old shipping labels on packages from previous shipments.

Amazon EasySell

While Fulfillment by Amazon is targeted at professional sellers, Amazon is also hoping to attract part-time, casual sellers. It's offering a re-branded version called EasySell, targeted at customers who want to turn their used books, videos and games into cash but don't want the hassle of selling it themselves.

Sellers pay monthly storage fees and can choose to have Amazon "dispose" of unsold items after 60 days. Monthly storage fees are 45 cents per cubic foot for the first six months, then 60 cents per month. However, storage fees are charged only for the actual size—an average DVD or CD would cost 2 cents per month in storage fees. The rates are offered only to individual sellers who don't have a Pro-Merchant account.

For more information on FBA, visit:

http://fba.amazon.com

Use Amazon as a drop-shipper

Another way to outsource business functions to Amazon is to enroll in its Drop Ship by Amazon program. With this program, you can sell Amazon items on your Web site in exchange for a percentage of the proceeds.

If you wish, you can restrict the product selection to certain products, if you want to offer only books and DVDs on your site, for example. With this program, the seller is responsible for customer support.

For more information, see:

http://www.amazonservices.com/dropship

Imports and exports

You can forward large import shipments to Amazon's fulfillment center as the final destination, but you must arrange for your own customs broker to handle this. Amazon won't act as the import consignee or final address in shipping from other countries. You must arrange a separate domestic shipment to Amazon's warehouse.

After your merchandise is at Amazon's fulfillment center, you can ask Amazon to export your products to another country, as long as Amazon agrees that the products are eligible for foreign shipment. Such a deal causes your products shipped to foreign addresses to pass to the recipient at the shipment point. There are other conditions too:

- Amazon may limit the total value of foreign-eligible products shipped to a single customer at a single foreign address in a single shipment. Amazon doesn't offer a service for filing the shipper's export declaration and assumes no liability regarding that function.

- Shipments to foreign addresses may not be returned, even if the customer requests it. Amazon may decide to abandon to the carrier a shipment to a foreign address that is refused or damaged.

Amazon won't calculate or display any taxes, duties or other assessments on orders for your products designated for shipment to foreign addresses.

Export items

If you decide to enable your FBA account for international sales, buyers outside of the United States can purchase your media items on www.amazon.com, and Amazon fulfills the order with the required export documentation submitted on your behalf. Enabling your account for international sales doesn't mean your items are listed on Amazon's international sites, such as Amazon.ca, Amazon.co.uk and others.

With FBA Export, you can export most media products—books, music, DVDs and videos—to all countries other than Canada. If you decide to use FBA Export, all of your media products are offered for export. You can't offer some of your items for export and others domestically only.

There is no extra cost for signing up for FBA Export; all the costs are included in fulfillment fees.

To participate in FBA Export, you'll need to send Amazon an image of a signature that it can use on the CN-22 Sender's Declaration, a Postal Service form. The person whose signature is used is responsible for verifying that the details in the declaration are correct, and that the items being exported don't contain items prohibited by postal or customs regulations.

Later, if you decide you no longer want to ship FBA orders internationally, you can withdraw from FBA Export.

Prepare items for shipment

Each FBA item you send to Amazon must have a label printed through Seller Central or the original scannable label showing the UPC or EAN. You can print labels through Seller Central onto label stock fed into a laser printer. The label will have the product description on it, helping you match the label with the right item. The label size supported by Amazon is 1" x 2-5/8", which can usually be found at office supply stores such as Staples or Office Depot. You can also purchase these labels on Amazon's Web site. The most popular label brand is Avery, but cheaper, no-name labels are available at much lower cost elsewhere on the Web.

After you register the type of product you're going to sell through FBA, you enter the number of units of that product type. You can enter this information through Seller Central or using third-party software designated by Amazon. You document the shipment in Seller Central, and after sending the packages, check "Mark as Shipped."

You can also arrange direct shipment of inventory to Amazon from suppliers, including those in foreign countries. Sellers with shipments originating in other countries must arrange import and customs clearance, then arrange for the delivery to Amazon's fulfillment center.

Amazon doesn't perform quality inspections when it receives FBA items from you. However, if an item is obviously damaged or destroyed during shipment, it's set aside as unsellable. If you described the item as "new" and there is apparent damage, such as cracks or tears, the item is set aside. However, if the item was described as "used" and has minor damage, Amazon assumes it arrived in the stated condition and makes it available to buyers.

Amazon might also identify an item as "unsellable" after it's been returned by a customer in a different condition than when it was shipped from the warehouse. Items marked "unsellable" are set aside for 90 days, during which you can request they be returned to you at your expense.

You can monitor your inventory levels and status of shipments through Seller Central. When an Amazon fulfillment center receives one of your FBA shipments, it aims to scan the shipment and make the items available within three business days of receipt. Processing time is extended to five business days during the holiday buying season. Sometimes shipments aren't processed during these timeframes for various reasons. According to Amazon, the primary causes of delayed shipment processing are:

- Poor-quality or missing labels, preventing accurate scans.

- Over- or under-shipments. A shipment with inaccurate quantities slows down processing because Amazon must research the issue.

- Poor packaging, loose product, and damaged items.

Compete with feedback

Sometimes it's easy to forget the importance of customer service during the heat of day-to-day selling chores. Because Amazon sellers and buyers aren't interacting face-to-face, Internet-based transactions can seem very impersonal. If you're selling exclusively on Amazon, most of the time you're selling to new customers. And even if you do sell to someone a second time, it's possible they won't remember your seller name anyway. So, you might wonder, how important is it to strive for excellent customer service when Amazon is providing a seemingly endless stream of new buyers? What does it matter if one in every 15 customers is unhappy with their transaction?

The answer is simple: If you're in business for the long haul and you want to be as competitive as possible, it's in your best interests to satisfy each customer. Striving for an excellent buying experience for all your customers is essential to the health of your business for two main reasons:

1. **To protect your business.** If you're selling at an online venue such as Amazon, you'll be more competitive if you can display a good feedback record. Many of the customers buying cheap items don't look at feedback, but those who buy expensive stuff do. The customers buying the high-end merchandise, the ones whose business is likely to be most profitable for you, want to deal with a seller who appears reliable and trustworthy. They will pay a premium to buy from a seller who has demonstrated reliability through an excellent feedback record.

2. **To make your business easier to manage.** Pay attention to the little things, like checking your e-mail and Seller Account page every few hours and being proactive about handling problems and customer complaints. If you can nip little problems in the bud, you can prevent a lot of big problems from happening. Big problems can be prevented at many stages along the way, but once they've mushroomed into a fiasco, they cost a tremendous amount of time and energy.

If you're new to selling, it might not be apparent yet, but you'll have plenty of repeat customers if you stick around long enough. It's no coincidence that the feedback of the most successful Amazon sellers is peppered with comments like, "Pleased again from buying from this seller." Make a customer happy once, and they will look for a reason to buy from you again.

Here's a good way to generate ideas on how you can improve your customer service: Make a few purchases yourself, and gauge your own satisfaction from your fellow Marketplace sellers. Are you willing to risk your own money on a seller with spotty feedback? How do others measure up regarding responsiveness, packing materials, and accuracy of descriptions? Compare the practices of these sellers with your own habits.

Moreover, good selling practices benefit us all. Every buyer that is happy with a purchase increases the odds that they'll buy again from Amazon, and recommend it to friends.

A good rule of thumb for customer service is to promptly answer all inquiries from customers, and to fulfill all the requests of customers whenever practical. However, if you're selling on Amazon, one request you can safely ignore if you wish is the occasional customer who asks to complete a transaction off-site using cash or PayPal. These customers will often complain that they don't like to buy things on the Internet (so why, then, are they shopping online?) or that they don't have a proper account.

It seems that sellers get this type of request more often when they are new, and this type of request becomes infrequent once you appear to be an established seller. Perhaps they think you'll offer them a great deal when you don't have to pay a commission or fees to an intermediary like Amazon. But is it really worth going out of your way to avoid paying a few dollars of commission? Amazon and all the selling venues prohibit off-site deals, and while it's unlikely, there's always the chance that somebody asking for an off-site deal would end up reporting you. Also, you should be concerned about getting a counterfeit check or ending up in some other type of scam. Using Amazon Payments and PayPal affords you some protection.

In any case, you can better spend your time finding and listing new merchandise for sale, rather than haggling with customers who want you to make a special deal or bend the rules.

Feedback ground rules

Feedback is the mechanism by which buyers and sellers can trust each other, despite unfamiliarity and the lack of physical contact. On Amazon, feedback consists of a five-star system, with five stars being the best possible rating; one star the worst:

5 (Excellent) ★★★★★
4 (Good) ★★★★☆
3 (Fair) ★★★☆☆
2 (Poor) ★★☆☆☆
1 (Awful) ★☆☆☆☆

On Amazon each buyer can rate a seller on each transaction. Twenty-one calendar days after the purchase, customers receive an e-mail request from Amazon to submit feedback.

If the buyer hasn't received the item, they might click **contact this seller** to ask about the order status. Otherwise, they can either ignore the e-mail (about 75 percent do) or click on the link **Leave seller feedback.**

Amazon's feedback reminder form is sent to buyers 21 calendar days after the order date.

The feedback submitted through these forms will become your reputation on Amazon, a way for buyers to gauge how prompt, honest and reliable your service is.

Before shopping with you, sellers can click on the stars accompanying your seller nickname to see a feedback summary like this:

Sellers who haven't yet received any feedback ratings have no score displayed, just a smiley face image and the text "Just Launched" next to their seller nickname.

Buyers sometime leave feedback before receiving the reminder e-mail from Amazon. At any time, buyers can follow a link to the feedback form from their **Open and recently shipped orders** section on Amazon. A **Rate your seller** link appears under the shipping address and shipping method details.

| | At a Glance | Feedback | Shipping Rates | Returns | Seller Help |

MediaCrazy
Feedback Rating: ★★★★☆
4.7 stars over the past 12 months (**4680** ratings)

Feedback	30 days	90 days	365 days	Lifetime
Positive:	85%	89%	92%	91%
Neutral:	3%	3%	2%	2%
Negative:	12%	8%	6%	7%
Count:	330	1241	4680	14997

What do these mean?

Recent Feedback: See all feedback

5 out of 5: "fast shippin and book is brand new"
Date: 2/12/2008   Rated by Buyer: IRWIN R.

5 out of 5: "It's all good."
Date: 2/12/2008   Rated by Buyer: ranger

4 out of 5: "Great price on a hard to find item."
Date: 2/12/2008   Rated by Buyer: Rich E.

5 out of 5: "Great Transaction."
Date: 2/12/2008   Rated by Buyer: Richard W.

5 out of 5: "thanks. Quick shipping etc..."
Date: 2/12/2008   Rated by Buyer: William S.

Note: feedback calculations only include ratings left by buyers.
                                  See all feedback

A-to-z Safe Buying Guarantee Protection
Place your merchant order through the Amazon.com Shopping Cart or 1-Click and your purchase is protected by the A-to-z Safe Buying Guarantee. Amazon.com automatically transfers your payment to the merchant so you'll never need to pay a merchant directly. Our A-to-z Safe Buying Guarantee covers both the delivery of your item and its condition upon receipt...read more

Marketplace Shipping Times
Sellers agree to ship within 2 business days of your purchase. Domestic Standard shipments are expected to arrive within 4 to 14 business days after shipping (they may take as long as 21 business days for media).
                                  See all shipping options

About Seller
MediaCrazy sells BRAND NEW movies (DVDs, CDs, Books, Video Games) at deeply discounted prices, backed up by OUTSTANDING CUSTOMER SERVICE! We ship from centers throughout the U.S. with delivery read more

Related Links:
· Contact this seller
· Help with ordering from Marketplace sellers

Your feedback as a merchant is on display at this summary page.

Before leaving negative feedback, buyers are urged to contact the seller first and try to resolve any differences. But too few buyers go to the trouble to do this, and sometimes leave critical feedback due to a simple misunderstanding.

Because all sellers are at risk of receiving the occasional undeserved negative feedback, the system is relatively fair—it rewards reliable sellers who communicate well with their customers. Sellers who fail to live up to their promises or don't communicate with their customers quickly suffer from the bad feedback ratings. It makes it tougher for them to make a sale, since educated buyers avoid sellers with poor track records.

Besides being shunned by buyers, you can expect to draw extra attention from Amazon if your feedback dips below a certain level. Amazon's performance targets state that "the number of negative feedback entries should be less than 5 percent of the total feedback entries received."

Keep a high feedback average

Sellers who are able to build a positive feedback record have a huge advantage over competitors and can command higher prices than lower-ranked competitors. So spending some time and energy maintaining a superior feedback record can help you improve your business over the long term.

Buyers who consult feedback ratings on Amazon Marketplace will concern themselves mainly with the "At a Glance" page, which summarizes the percentages for positive, negative, and neutral ratings for sellers over four time periods: 30 days, 90 days, 365 days and lifetime. A perfect score is 100, and careful sellers can expect to keep their positive feedback averages in the mid-90s on Amazon. Sellers gripe about feedback systems, which are always imperfect, but feedback can serve as a useful tool for managing your business. By aiming to minimize negative feedback, you'll automatically be focused on preventing mistakes that cost money to correct. Negative feedback can help you identify problems with your business.

Careful Amazon sellers have a variety of methods for maintaining a good feedback record. Some of these methods can minimize your short-term profits but help your business in the long run by burnishing your image as a trusted party:

- **Prompt shipping.** Buyers expect prompt shipment and a confirmation of shipment. Part-time sellers can probably get by shipping two or three times per week, but if you take your business seriously, commit yourself to shipping on a daily basis. Nothing invites negative feedback from customers more than a lackadaisical approach to shipment times.

- **Aim higher than the minimum requirements.** Justified or not, more than half of buyer feedback comments will mention the delivery time. "Prompt delivery" and "I received it in a few days" are typical feedback comments from satisfied customers. "Very slow" is a typical feedback comment, and obviously, the customer could actually be rating the Postal Service rather than the seller. The more promptly you ship, the less likely buyers are to complain.

• **Upgrade shipping for buyers outside the continental U.S.** Buyers of media items frequently complain about tardy delivery when sellers use Postal Service Media Mail, which can take three weeks or more to arrive. Delivery can take even longer for buyers in Alaska, Hawaii, or U.S. government personnel at overseas locations. Don't take a chance with Media Mail for these buyers—upgrade to First Class Mail or a Priority Mail flat rate envelope for buyers outside the lower 48 states.

• **Avoid international shipping on heavy items.** If you can't afford airmail shipping for overseas buyers, don't offer the item for international sale. Although Amazon's Web site clearly explains that international shipments can take a month or more, too many overseas buyers don't read the fine print. Particularly if you are selling items at small profit margins, don't risk your feedback to overseas buyers unless you can ensure delivery within 10 days.

• **Send a shipment confirmation.** Acknowledge your shipments with a message confirming the shipment. This prevents time-consuming, needless inquiries from buyers curious about the order status days later. Your shipment confirmations can be automated.

• **Describe items accurately.** Be conservative when describing any imperfections of your merchandise. A customer who feels cheated is likely to leave a vindictive feedback rating. Manage your customers' expectations by giving them all the facts they need for their buying decision.

• **Provide your contact information.** A packing slip with the order number and your e-mail address will be useful in case you made a mistake filling the order or the customer ordered the wrong item. If the customer can't figure out how to contact you quickly, they're more likely to communicate via negative feedback.

• **Be generous when correcting your mistakes.** If a customer has to return an item due to your mistake, it's a good idea to refund a percentage of the sale to compensate for the inconvenience.

Seller performance targets

To ensure that sellers meet certain minimum standards, Amazon sets seller performance targets. Failure to meet these targets can bring your account extra scrutiny and sometimes leads to warnings or suspensions of selling privileges.

- **Feedback:** The number of negative feedback entries should be less than 5 percent of the total feedback entries received.

- **A-to-Z Guarantee Claim Rate:** The number of Guarantee claims should be less than 0.5 percent of orders received.

- **Refund Rate:** The number of refunded media units in a calendar month should be less than 5 percent of the number of media units sold.

Feedback removal

Amazon removes feedback in only two circumstances:

- The feedback includes obscene language.

- The feedback includes personal information, such as a person's full name or telephone number.

However, it is possible for buyers to remove feedback they've left. Here are simple instructions to give your buyers who agree to remove feedback:

1. Go to **http://www.amazon.com/your-account**
2. Find the pull-down menu next to View by Order. Select **Orders placed in the past 6 months** and hit the "go" button.
3. After you sign in, you'll see a list of your recent orders. Select the relevant order and click the **View order** button.
4. You will find a feedback section two-thirds of the way down the page. To remove feedback, click on the **Remove** link in the feedback section of the order summary.
5. You may only remove feedback if it is 60 days or less since you left the feedback.

If you have the Amazon order number handy, you can replace the first three steps described above with a URL you can supply to your customer. To build the URL, add the order ID into this link:

https://www.amazon.com/gp/css/summary/edit.html?orderI D=(insert order id here)

Buyers to whom you have refunded money for any reason, such as a stock-out or a returned item, may still leave feedback on your account. So it pays to process returns and refunds promptly and courteously.

Respond to negative feedback

When you receive a negative or neutral feedback, there are four possible courses of action:

1. **Learn a lesson and let it go:** Negative feedback is a great opportunity to learn about and improve your operational practices. Consider what went wrong to prompt the buyer to leave negative feedback, fix the underlying problems in your business, and let your good record stand for itself.

2. **Ask the buyer to remove the feedback:** If you want to respond to negative feedback, the best option is to work with the buyer to improve the situation that led to the negative feedback. Then, ask the buyer to remove the feedback. To do this, e-mail the buyer with concern over the problem, and remedy it if possible. If you develop a positive relationship, ask the buyer to remove the feedback. When contacting a buyer, always keep in mind that pressuring a buyer is unacceptable and a violation of Community Rules.

3. **Leave a response to the feedback.** If the buyer doesn't cooperate in removing the feedback, leave a professional and positive comment in response to the feedback, and move on. To do this, go to the Seller Account and click **View your live Auctions Member Profile** under the **Account Settings** heading. Once there, click **See all seller feedback**. When you find the feedback you would like to respond to, click the link to

respond to the feedback. You'll be able to remove the response later if you like, and if your buyer eventually decides to remove the feedback, your response will automatically be removed.

4. **Leave feedback for the buyer:** You may leave feedback for the buyer. This option may produce some momentary satisfaction but is largely a waste of time, since few buyers or sellers consult buyer feedback records.

Q&A: Should I refund my irate customer?

QUESTION: It looks like I made a rookie error and listed an item in the wrong place on Amazon. I must have entered the product ID incorrectly. Anyway, the customer didn't get the item they expected, so I received an angry message.

My issue is this: This customer is demanding an immediate refund or she will give me very negative feedback. She wants the refund before she returns the item. I am happy to refund her, but not until the item is returned to me. She's holding me hostage by threatening my 100 percent positive feedback record.

I don't believe she has the right to demand a refund before she returns the product. Would a brick-and-mortar store refund your money if you hadn't returned the item yet? Of course not. They aren't going to refund and wait for the product to be returned two weeks later.

Who is right?

ANSWER: Sometimes you've got to forget about "who is right." I understand the quandary you're in. Not a week goes by when there isn't some goof-up I've got to fix. Unfortunately, mistakes happen, and I ship the wrong item to a customer at least three or four times a month, out of the several hundred orders I process.

Fortunately, buyers often give you the benefit of the doubt, as long as you handle the situation professionally. I've handled this type of situation both ways—by demanding the item back first, and at other times I've refunded first, giving the customer the benefit of the doubt.

Here's my basic advice—if the item is worth less than $25, give the customer an immediate refund and accept the return later. This has been satisfactory every time I've tried it. And of course, apologize profusely to the customer, and emphasize that the error was unintentional.

I keep a log of everyone I've refunded for any reason. So far nobody's ever tried for a second refund.

You've got to be just as diplomatic at those times when the customer has made an error, too. And one thing to remember about people who buy stuff online: They *always* think they're in the right, even when they're wrong. Once they have that idea in their head there's nothing we the seller can do to change that idea, we've just got to make the best of things.

Treat customers the way you'd like to be treated yourself.

Excerpted from Steve Weber's "Selling Books" blog.

See your feedback summary

Buyers can click on your seller nickname to view your lifetime feedback as well as summaries for three periods—30 days, 90 days and 365 days—at your "At a Glance Feedback" page. Here, buyers can read your past five feedback comments. They can also click a link to view your entire seller feedback history.

Until sellers have more than 10 ratings over the past 365 days, the lifetime rating are displayed instead.

Some types of feedback ratings are ignored when Amazon computes your feedback score:

• Ratings you may have earned as a buyer aren't included; only your feedback from your customers is counted. Comments and ratings from sellers you've transacted with are visible, but the ratings don't count toward your score.

• Feedback from other international marketplaces. For example, if you primarily sell in the UK using Amazon.co.uk, you can't use your UK feedback on Amazon's U.S. or Canadian site. On the other hand, a negative feedback in Japan won't hurt your score as a U.S. seller.

• Buyers have a 90-day window during which they can leave feedback. If they leave feedback, they have 60 days after that point during which they can remove that feedback rating.

View feedback for a buyer

All sellers may leave feedback for their buyers, but seldom do. However, if you have concerns about a buyer, viewing the feedback can alert you to the fact that other sellers have experienced problems with a buyer in the past. Here's how to view feedback for a buyer:

1. Go to your Seller Account page:

http://amazon.com/seller-account

2. Click on **Search your Marketplace** orders and locate the order from the buyer in question.
3. Click the order ID to view order details.
4. To see the buyer's feedback, click on their name.
5. On the buyer's member profile page, click **See all seller feedback.** The total number listed by the name is based on feedback received as a seller, so you'll want to click through even if the number is zero.
6. Click on the link and you'll see any feedback left for the buyer.

Leave feedback for buyers

You are welcome to leave feedback for your buyers. Most buyers do not read their feedback, and Amazon does not use buyer feedback to evaluate buyers. This functionality may be useful if you want to help future sellers identify a difficult buyer. You should not feel compelled to leave feedback for all buyers.

Here's how to leave feedback for a buyer:

1. Go to your Seller Account

http://amazon.com/seller-account

2. Click on **Search your Marketplace orders** and locate the relevant order.

3. Click the order ID to view order details.
4. Then click the **Leave buyer feedback** button.
5. You can only leave feedback for orders placed less than 90 days ago.

Handle non-delivery reports

If you sell on Amazon long enough, you'll have cases where the customer doesn't receive the item even though you shipped it promptly. Mistakes can happen at several points along the way, and when a mishap occurs, you have three options:

- **Refunding the buyer.** If the item is inexpensive, sometimes the best course is to refund. If the order does turn up eventually, Amazon can recharge the customer if they authorize it.

- **Shipping a replacement or drop-shipping an order.** This causes a loss for your business, but results in customer goodwill.

- **Asking the buyer to wait longer.** If the item was sent via U.S. Postal Service standard mail less than 30 days ago, it's possible that the item is still en route. You might ask the customer to wait until the 30-day point, promising to refund or ship a replacement if the original item hasn't arrived at that time. If you choose this route, your customer has the option of filing an A-to-Z Guarantee claim against your account.

Returns and restocking fees

Amazon authorizes buyers to return new media items (books, CDs, and videos) in original condition. The buyer must postmark their return package within 30 days of your shipment. Sellers are allowed to charge a "reasonable" restocking fee of no more than 20 percent. However, if the item was returned because it was defective, damaged, or "materially different" than advertised, you should not charge any restocking fee.

- **Used media items.** The buyer is obligated to report any damage, defects or material difference to you within seven days of receipt. Again, returns must be postmarked within 30 days of shipment.

- **Software.** If you sell software in new condition and the item has been opened, you may refuse to accept the return unless the product was defective. If you advertised it as a used item and it was not materially different, you can refuse the return. However, if the item is materially different, returns should be accepted when received back in the original condition, postmarked within 30 days of shipment.

- **Electronics.** When items shipped new and unopened are returned, Amazon expects sellers to accept the return and charge a "reasonable" restocking fee of about 15 percent. But if the item is used and arrives damaged or defective, the buyer must report this to you within seven days of receipt and negotiate how it will be returned. If the item is found defective more than 30 days after shipment and is covered by a warranty, sellers are supposed to "assist" buyers in making a warranty claim with the manufacturer.

Electronics sellers are required to accept returns, even if the item was just as described. If the seller declines the return of an item sold for less than $300 and Amazon decides that it was "materially different," Amazon may deduct the funds from your account if the buyer files an A-to-Z Guarantee claim.

Q&A: Do canceled orders hurt sellers?

QUESTION: My bookstore sells textbooks on Amazon. I'm worried that our performance summary rating on Amazon is going to suffer because we get quite a few order cancellations from students buying textbooks, especially at semester breaks.

Amazon's threshold for refunds is 5 percent. Today we've had 100 Amazon Marketplace orders but five cancellations before the books shipped. We're not getting any reasons for the cancellations, just e-mails asking to cancel.

I think this is a double-edged sword—we're apt to get negative feedback for some unknown reason, and we're worried about our account being suspended by Amazon's "Seller Performance" department for an excessive refund rate.

Should I call Amazon's customer service number to try to explain the situation so they don't kick us off? If so, what number should we call?

ANSWER: Your performance summary provides statistics on your sales, refunds, customer feedback, and A-to-Z Guarantee claims. I remember when Amazon began compiling this data in 2003, there was a big hubbub because they e-mailed the first few monthly tallies to the sellers, even sellers with good records. Many sellers felt compelled to contest each and every ding on their records. Very soon afterward, Amazon quit mailing those monthly statistics. But they're still monitoring the numbers, and if your account is outside the norm, you can bet you'll hear about it.

Honestly, I wouldn't be too concerned about one day of excessive refunds. I doubt your refund rate is out of line compared to other sellers who do heavy volume in textbook selling. I'm sure Amazon sees a spike in refunds across the board during the textbook buying seasons. Students are notorious for buying the wrong edition, dropping classes, etc. I always get a lot of cancellations without explanations from students too.

Another problem with student buyers is that they rarely pay for "expedited" shipping but they are always in a hurry to receive the book. So some of your student buyers may be canceling after they receive their order confirmation e-mail from Amazon, which explains that standard Marketplace media shipments can take more than three weeks to arrive due to USPS Media Mail. One way you can help prevent this is to add this language to your condition comments for textbooks: "We recommend "Expedited" shipping at checkout for prompt delivery."

Established sellers receive a warning if their performance summary deteriorates. Newer sellers may have their account suspended immediately. If you want to discuss this with someone at Amazon, my best advice would be to call the seller support line and ask to speak with a supervisor: 1-877-251-0696

Excerpted from Steve Weber's "Selling Books" blog.

Chargebacks and A-to-Z claims

Sometimes dissatisfied customers will file an A-to-Z guarantee claim with Amazon, and sometimes customers will dispute the transaction with their credit card company, a process known as a "chargeback." Other times, chargebacks are filed after unauthorized use of the credit card.

In any case, Amazon will contact you, asking for details about the transaction, although there are some differences. Buyers can initiate a chargeback with their credit card company at any time, from the day following the transaction until many months later. Although Amazon investigates the chargeback, the resolution is determined by the buyer's card issuer.

A-to-Z claims can only be filed in a certain time window. The earliest time buyers can file a claim is three calendar days after the maximum estimated delivery date, or 30 days from the order date. The latest time that buyers can file an A-to-Z claim is 90 days after the transaction.

Marketplace buyers are limited to a lifetime total of five A-to-Z claims.

A-to-Z claims cover buyers in two situations:

- The item fails to arrive.

- The item is materially different than expected.

After the buyer submits an A-to-Z claim, the seller receives an automated e-mail from Amazon asking for the seller's version of the events, the date of shipment, and a tracking number.

When customers submit a claim for an order that was not fulfilled by the seller, the seller should issue a refund immediately. Amazon denies A-to-Z claims when the seller has already refunded the customer or the buyer has initiated a chargeback with their credit card issuer.

Sometimes Amazon reimburses the customer while investigating a claim, but waits until hearing from the seller before deciding whether the seller is responsible.

Take care to minimize the number of A-to-Z claims against your account where possible because an excessive number of claims can result in suspension or closure of your account.

Sellers can monitor their performance summary at this page:
www.amazon.com/gp/seller-account/seller-performance/summary.html

To manage your A-to-Z claims from your Seller Account page, click on the **A-to-Z Guarantee Claims** link.

The best way to guard against guarantee claims and chargebacks against your account is to ship promptly with a tracking number, and ship only to the address provided by Amazon. For high-value transactions, it's prudent to require a signature upon receipt of the package—a service that can be provided by the Postal Service and most other carriers, although it costs extra in some cases. You should retain all your shipping records for at least six months in case of an inquiry.

If you receive an A-to-Z or chargeback e-mail from Amazon, the subject line will include the words, "Your immediate attention required." Here is the text of a chargeback notification:

Greetings from Amazon Payments.

We are writing to let you know that the credit card issuer has contacted us on behalf of the purchaser of the below transaction. We would ask that you provide us with proof of delivery to provide to the credit card issuer.

Items Purchased:
Shipping Address:

Please reply to this email and type "X" in the applicable box (e.g.,[X]).
*Please check only one box.

[ ] Media Mail

[ ] Trackable shipping method (Please check this box only if item shipped Media Mail, but with a tracking number) Please also provide us with the date the order was shipped, the tracking number (if applicable) and any other information pertinent to the claim in the box below:

Please note that failure to respond to this inquiry within seven (7) days of this e-mail with sufficient information may result in a debit to your Amazon Payments account up to the amount of the transaction.

We appreciate your cooperation in helping resolve this matter and look forward to receiving your reply.

Thank you for choosing Amazon.com.

Amazon.com Customer Service
http://www.amazon.com

Seller accounts are debited for chargebacks in service-related incidents, such as non-receipt and material difference of merchandise. Amazon covers claims for payment-related chargebacks, such as stolen cards and other payment fraud. Amazon informs you of the outcome of an investigation only when you are held responsible for the chargeback.

Amazon Seller Performance

Amazon's Seller Performance department (previously known as "Amazon Alliance") polices Marketplace by kicking off unethical sellers—those caught selling pirated products or those who have excessive refunds or A-to-Z claims. Another thing Seller Performance screens for is "duplicate" accounts—Marketplace sellers that share a common mailing address, Internet address, or some other detail. The thinking is that someone who opens a "duplicate" or "linked" account was probably shut down previously for poor business practices, and is trying to start over on Amazon with a clean slate.

Generally this system works pretty well, and is one of the reasons the typical Marketplace buying experience is positive. The problem is, there's no apparent communications channel when Seller Performance makes a mistake. Apparently Amazon screens seller accounts for duplicate phone numbers, or addresses, and when they find a match, they disable your account and send a message like this:

> Greetings from Amazon.com.
>
> This message is to inform you that we have blocked your Amazon.com Auctions and Marketplace account. Your open listings have been cancelled and you are no longer able to sell on our site.
>
> We have taken this action because it has come to our attention that this account is related to an account which has been previously blocked for violations of our Community Rules.
>
> While we do not provide detailed information on how we link related accounts, we have thoroughly reviewed our records and confirmed that we have significant evidence that this account is related to another account previously closed for community rules violations.

If you still have items to ship, please take appropriate steps to resolve your pending sales. Your Seller Account will remain accessible and you are encouraged to refund or ship pending orders.

Your funds are on temporary hold for 90 days from the date of your final sale. After 90 days, the funds will be disbursed, provided we do not receive chargebacks or A-to-Z Guarantee claims against your sales. If you have further questions about your disbursement, please email payments-funds@amazon.com.

While we appreciate your interest, please understand that the closure of an account is a permanent action. Any subsequent accounts that are opened will be closed as well. Thank you for your understanding with our decision.

Regards,

Item and Seller Quality

Amazon.com

http://www.amazon.com

If Seller Performance shuts down your account erroneously, you'll need to try several avenues of communication to get your account restored:

1. Call Seller Support at 1-877-251-0696. Ask to speak with a supervisor.

2. Write an e-mail to seller-performance@amazon.com. In reply, you'll receive an automated message indicating that Amazon's "seller performance team" received your message.

Some sellers have reported that their accounts were erroneously flagged after they logged into their seller account at a public library. So it's best to use your seller account only on your home computer.

Also, beware of messages that purport to be from Amazon Seller Performance or Amazon Alliance but are actually a "phishing" message from a computer hacker. Such phishing e-mails may claim that your account has been suspended and use identical language as Amazon's notifications. That is why it's best to telephone Amazon's Seller Support staff immediately and verify the issue. The phishing e-mails usually have a link, which you should not click on, nor should you enter any of your account information. Scammers who are successful at this can gain access to your account, divert your payments to their own bank accounts, and enter fraudulent listings onto Amazon Marketplace using your seller name.

Q&A: Should I ask buyers for feedback?

QUESTION: I've been selling online since 1999, but started getting serious about selling on Amazon a year ago. My feedback is small, only four ratings. Should I ask for feedback on Amazon?

ANSWER: My thinking on this has evolved a bit in the past few years. Originally, I rigged up a system to send my Amazon customers an e-mail shipping confirmation, including a link for leaving feedback. This way I'd often receive feedback before the customer received the 21-day reminder e-mail from Amazon.

I solicited feedback, of course, because I think having a long, positive track record makes you more competitive as a seller, making it more likely that people will buy from you.

I changed my mind on this some months ago. I realized that perhaps half of the negative feedback ratings I was getting was before the 21-day mark. Almost always, it was someone frustrated about slow delivery of USPS Media Mail. Eventually I decided that I could avoid a lot of that negative feedback by not asking for the feedback at the time of shipment. It's just a guess, but I figure that most of those people who are angry about slow delivery at the 10-day mark won't be angry after they receive their item and get Amazon's 21-day reminder to leave feedback—and, hopefully they won't leave negative feedback.

If you're trying to build up your feedback, just continue what you're doing, perhaps ramp up your selling a bit. There is software available for automating the process of asking for feedback, but I really don't think it's worth it. I base this idea on my own buying behavior when I'm shopping on Marketplace. All else being equal, I will usually buy from a seller who has a better average score (I like to see 95 percent positive) instead of a seller with more feedback but more negatives. In other words, when my own money is at risk, I'll buy from a seller with 96 percent positive and 200 total ratings before buying from someone who has 2,000 feedbacks but only 92 percent positive.

Sellers can leave feedback for buyers too on Amazon, but it's a convoluted process and hardly worth the trouble. Perhaps 99 percent of Marketplace buyers aren't aware of buyer feedback and don't care.

Buyer feedback was important back when Amazon first launched third-party selling, and a lot of the buyers had experience on eBay. Nowadays, most Marketplace buyers are mainstream consumers. Many are unfamiliar with eBay, have never purchased from an individual online before, and some of them don't even realize that a Marketplace purchase isn't being shipped directly from Amazon.

So over time, I've gotten a lot more relaxed in my attitude toward feedback. Lately I just take care of my business the best I can, and hope the feedback situation takes care of itself.

Excerpted from Steve Weber's "Selling Books" blog.

Best practices

Amazon prescribes these "best practices" for customer service:

- Answer all buyer inquiries within 24 hours of receipt. Good communication with buyers promotes good feedback for sellers.

- Marketplace customers expect the same level of service from third-party sellers as they do when buying directly from Amazon. Be proactive, meet and exceed expectations, and use Amazon's reputation for customer service to your advantage.

Explore the social jungle

Internet social networking is closely watched by sellers of all types because it can provide effective, free advertising for all sorts of products. The conventional wisdom is that Web. 2.0 and social networking tools burst into the popular culture a couple of years ago with the emergence of MySpace.com. In fact, Amazon.com was a pioneering—and by far the most widely used—user of social networking features and purveyor of "user-generated" content. In fact, Amazon's most valuable feature may be the product reviews submitted by users.

Amazon has all the features of most social-networking sites such as MySpace, and then some. If your product is sold on the site—or if related items are sold there—Amazon can be a valuable platform.

Get crazy with lists

Listmania lists allow any Amazon user—customers, authors, sellers, music lovers, movie buffs—to create lists of their favorite items organized by theme. Listmanias appear in various places on Amazon, like product detail pages and alongside search results. Listmanias that mention your product can expose it to thousands of potential customers on Amazon, and the list can even appear in Google search results for associated keywords.

Listmanias are ranked by popularity among shoppers, based on viewership and the number of votes calling it "helpful." For example, one popular list is dedicated to novelist Nick Hornby, and was compiled by one of his fans. Under each novel is a pithy quote from the Listmania author, just enough to convey the gist of each book and why it appears. The list includes most of Hornby's books, other books Hornby edited or wrote introductions for, and a few other novels by writers with similar styles. See this list at:

http://www.Amazon.com/gp/richpub/listmania/ fullview/1X1GGDBXARHZ6

See the 100 most popular Listmanias here:

http://www.Amazon.com/gp/richpub/listmania/toplists

Niche products stand to gain the most from Listmanias. The more focused a Listmania is, the more helpful it is to buyers hungry for specific information—so the more likely it is to be noticed, read carefully, and acted on. Niche Listmanias have less competition—Amazon can show only so many "Harry Potter" Listmanias while the thousands of similar lists wait in a queue. But your Listmania about "Organic Strawberries" may pop up in front of every single customer looking for relevant products.

To write a Listmania, click on the link at the bottom of your Amazon profile page, "More to Explore." Or start your list by clicking on the link **Create Your Own List** on an existing Listmania. Then:

1. Go to your Amazon Profile at: **www.Amazon.com/gp/pdp**.
2. Near the bottom of the middle column, in the section **More to Explore**, click **Listmania Lists**.
3. Click **Create your first one now** or **Create another list**.
4. Enter a title for your list and enter your "qualifications" such as "business owner" or "consultant." For your title, think of a blurb that will catch the eye of anyone shopping for a related item.
5. Enter products sold on Amazon, including your own, and write a short comment for each.
6. Click the **Preview** button and check for typos.
7. Edit your list, and when satisfied, click the button **Publish list**. You can edit it later if you wish.

Your Listmania lists will appear on your Amazon Profile and in search results related to items on your list. From your Profile, you'll have the option of editing your lists or deleting them.

So You'd Like to . . . guides

Have you ever wished you could submit a how-to essay to your local newspaper that demonstrates your expertise and helps publicize your business or product? You can accomplish much the same feat on Amazon by writing a *So You'd Like to ...* guide, which could be read by more people than a newspaper article.

Amazon's *So You'd Like to ...* guides somewhat resemble Listmania, but are more like tutorials. They're time-consuming and require considerably more original writing than Listmanias, but are consulted often, especially in niche topics. Some rewritten content from your blog or Web site might serve as the basis of a guide.

For example, you could write a guide called "Beginner's Guide to Growing Organic Fruit." In the course of writing your guide, you can link to items from Amazon's garden section and general gardening reference books.

To include products in your guide you'll need to look up their 10-digit ASIN (Amazon Standard Identification Number) that appears on the item's detail page under the heading **Product Details**.

To get started writing a guide, go to your Amazon profile at **www.Amazon.com/gp/pdp**. Near the bottom of the middle column, in the section labeled **More to Explore**, click on **So You'd Like to ... Guides**, then click on **Create a guide**. Guides must include at least three products sold on Amazon and may have a maximum of 50. The first three mentioned in your guide will become featured items that appear at the top of your guide when it appears on Amazon's site.

Break up your guide into sections every few paragraphs by inserting a subheading like this:

<HEADLINE: (Type your headline here)>

Before finishing, copy your text into a word processor and spell-check it. After you're finished writing and editing your guide, click on the **Publish** button.

Later you can add more products or content to your guides by editing them. From your Profile at **www.Amazon.com/gp/pdp**, click **So You'd Like to ... Guides** near the bottom of the middle column, then click the **Edit** button on the right of the guide you wish to change.

Write product reviews

No matter what you're selling on Amazon, a major factor will be the type of reviews it attracts from buyers. Good reviews can boost sales of the products you carry, and of course poor reviews can hurt sales. When you're considering what items to acquire for your inventory, always consult the Amazon user reviews to see which items are most popular.

You can also write reviews on Amazon yourself. Writing a compelling review can expose many thousands of Amazon shoppers to your name and your products. Of course if you have a continuing financial interest in the items you're reviewing, you should fully disclose any conflicts of interest in your review.

If your product is sold on Amazon, you can insert a link to its product page in your reviews of other items. Keep in mind that this will be considered self-serving by some observers. In no circumstances should you hide your identity or fail to mention any financial interest you may have with the products you're discussing.

Many Amazon reviewers add a plug for their product or business within their Amazon pen name, which is displayed with the reviews, such as "Thomas Edison, inventor of the light bulb."

To change the way your pen name is displayed, visit your Amazon Profile at **www.Amazon.com/gp/pdp**. In the left column, in the **About Me** section, click **change name**.

To write an Amazon product review, go to the product's detail page and scroll down to the section **Customer Reviews,** then click the button **Create your own review.** The maximum length of reviews is 1,000 words, and the recommended length is 75 to 300 words. The title of your review is limited to 60 characters.

Amazon strongly discourages the following elements in customer reviews:

- Dates of promotional tours or lectures that become outdated.

- Commenting on previous reviews (other reviews might be edited or deleted in the future).

- Profanity or cruel remarks.

- Single-word reviews.

- Contact information such as phone numbers, addresses or URLs.

- Discussing the item's price, availability, or shipping information.

- Asking people to "vote" for your review.

Check your review for spelling and typos by running the text through a word processor. Break up your text with a blank line between each paragraph to add white space.

Often reviews show up immediately on the product's detail page, but sometimes it takes several days. To ask about the status of a review, write to **community-help@amazon.com**.

The more helpful your review is to Amazon users, the more often it will be voted "helpful" and have an impact. "Most helpful" reviews have the most impact since they appear first.

Get credible with peers

Successful products have lots of positive reviews on Amazon, and it's no coincidence. It's another point in the positive feedback loop: Good products garner good reviews, which leads to more sales. Good reviews on Amazon are particularly crucial for new items and niche products.

Positive reviews on Amazon boost your sales not only on Amazon, but everywhere people buy consumer goods. What percentage of buyers at brick-and-mortar stores actually made their choice by reading

Amazon customer reviews? There's no way of knowing exactly, but rest assured it's a substantial and growing number.

Amazon's reviews are effective because they're often written by people who are knowledgeable and passionate about the item. On the whole, they're seen as an objective evaluation from someone with no ax to grind. Sure, many inept and biased reviews appear, but they're outweighed by the good ones.

Amazon tags

Internet "tags" are a brief description of something—a book, a Web site, or anything else found on the Web—assigned by an online community of users. For example, an Amazon user might give the tag "mystery novel" to a book by Agatha Christie. Perhaps thousands of other Amazon users will do the same thing, confirming the judgment.

Why should you care about tags? Because tags are an important new way for readers to discover your merchandise. Tagging is an individual activity with global utility. Each product listed for sale on Amazon.com, for example, can be assigned its own unique "category" yet reside in thousands of other categories at the same time.

Amazon added its tagging feature in 2005, and made it more prominent—higher on product detail pages—than its traditional category lists. Amazon tags are publicly viewable unless users designate them as private. You can manage your tags through a **Your Tags** field at the bottom of every Amazon page. Too see the tags people have given to any product on Amazon, scroll down the item's detail page to the line **Tags Customers Associate with This Product.**

Users create tags for their own purposes, but they can be used by anyone. With enough people participating, tags can become an effortless, super-accurate recommendations system among like-minded people. The site that popularized tagging was **www.Flickr.com**, a social site where users store, organize and share their digital photos. Instead of using a single category for organizing pictures—like a folder labeled "2005 Vacation"—members use one- or two-word tags like waterfall, solar eclipse, Houston, Joe or 2005. This way, photos can be grouped and discovered in multiple ways.

Tags are a form of *metadata*, which means, literally, "data about data." Tagging creates a *folksonomy*, a bottom-up method of categorization. *Taxonomies* are governed by experts like librarians and botanists who want to show hierarchical relationships. Folksonomies are built by amateurs but can be more helpful for users.

If you have a product sold on Amazon, you can increase its visibility by adding the obvious keywords appropriate to that product. For example, one of the digital cameras for sale on Amazon has 60 tags, including:

- Canon
- image stabilization
- powershot
- compact
- cam for Mary
- wide-angle

Amazon tags are indexed by Google and other search engines. As users of Amazon and other retailing sites begin to use tagging, finding niche products will become easier than ever. Tags assigned to obscure products will be rare but instantly apparent. A few common tags will be used by huge numbers of users and visible to everyone: The five most-used tags on Amazon are *DVD*, *music*, *books*, *fantasy* and *anime*. Most tags, including the more useful ones, will be seldom used, such as *bizarre apocalpytacism*, Amazon's least-used tag. Many tags will be used by just a few people, perhaps assigned to only one product, enabling a niche of one.

As a consumer, here are some ways you might use tags on Amazon:

- **To organize your books.** Tag the books you already own and organize them as you wish. If you don't agree with the category groups as Amazon has arranged them, make up your own. Tag the items that matter to you with categories you care about.

- **To remember merchandise you're considering buying.** If one of your tagged items is intended for a Christmas gift, you can tag the book "Xmas" or "present"—although those tags aren't very useful to others. Tags like "real best picture of 2004" are better.

- **Personalized recommendations based on tags.** Go to **www.Amazon.com/yourstore** and click on tags shown under the heading "Recommendations Based on Your Tags."

- You can view all your tags on Amazon here: **www.Amazon.com/gp/tagging/manage-tags**

Here you can add or delete tags, and designate them public or private. You can also edit or remove tags you've created by clicking on **Edit** from the product's Amazon page.

You can view the tags for any Amazon customer who's made at least one purchase, unless they've chosen to keep their tags private.

Tag-based marketing

As a marketer, you should use tags to stay current on how people are finding and sharing information in your product field. For example, you can subscribe to RSS feeds to monitor how consumers tag information related to your area of business. For example, to keep tabs on products related to organic fruit, you could bookmark this page:

http://del.icio.us/tag/organic+fruit

By bookmarking this page, you'll get updates on interesting links consumers are discovering and sharing about "organic fruit." You'll have a global focus group working for you 24 hours a day, seven days a week.

Or let's imagine you want to monitor all the books to which Amazon users assign the tag "murder mystery." You can watch:

www.Amazon.com/ gp/tagging/glance/murder+mystery

Should you tag your own products? Certainly, but anyone using tags for marketing should be transparent about it, says Steve Rubel, author of the blog Micro Persuasion. In other words, if you're plugging your own products, don't pretend you're an uninterested bystander. Don't hide your identity, and don't spam.

Problems with tags

One weakness of tags is that the same tag can mean two completely different things to different people. For example, one book, a memoir by CNN correspondent Anderson Cooper, is tagged by various Amazon users with "news memoir," "blue eyes," and "hunk." Since "hunk" is a tag with many possible meanings, it appears on many products with seemingly no connection—like a movie starring Russell Crowe, the DVD *Forrest Gump*, heavy sweaters, and books about the "chunky" clothing style.

Conversely, various people will assign different tags to the same thing—one person may tag photos of their dog "cocker spaniel" while another user tags the same photo "canines." A search for the tag "dogs" might not turn up either photo. With books, an Amazon user may assign the tag "Christmas" to a book about baseball, meaning that she intends to buy it as a Christmas gift. Meanwhile, customers using the tag "Christmas" to search for Christmas books will be frustrated.

Like any valuable tool, tags can be abused, too. If tagging goes mainstream, spammers will try exploiting tags by adding their irrelevant tags to popular items.

Tags aren't necessarily linked with semantics. So the word "blow" could be used as a tag for wind, cocaine, sucking, breath, or a picture of a tornado, or the sound of air rushing. The user of the tag, not a search engine, decides how the meaning fits for them.

Advocates of tagging assert these fears are overblown. With enough users, tags become self-correcting, so inappropriate or useless tags will be drowned out by the good ones.

Amazon tags for search

There's another kind of tag on Amazon that is more directly connected with the site's searching procedure. Amazon "Tags for Search" (formerly called "Search Suggestions") enables anyone with an Amazon account—seller or buyer—to add a bit of human intelligence to the site's search engine. On each product detail page, the link **Help others find this product—tag it for Amazon** allows users to recommend tying a product to specific keywords. Users also explain why the keywords are relevant and will help people find the item.

Let's imagine your company makes custom-built stands for televisions. You could suggest the term "HDTV" for your products. That way, Amazon shoppers searching for high-definition TVs could also discover your products.

You can take advantage of Search Suggestions by linking your product with relevant words and expressions that don't appear in the title. For example, let's imagine you sell a book about predicting hurricanes. A year after your book goes on the market, the most damaging hurricane in history, a storm named Zelda, devastates the Florida coast. By entering the Search Suggestion "Hurricane Zelda," more buyers would find your book, even though it didn't contain "Zelda."

Once your Search Suggestion is approved, when customers search using your keywords, the product appears in search results along with your relevancy **explanation.**

Make friends at the River

Amazon's "friends" feature resembles the friendship feature on MySpace and other networking sites, and is gaining prominence as Amazon increasingly emphasizes its "community" aspects. Designating someone your Amazon friend provides an easy way for you to track his or her community participation on Amazon. Depending on the privacy settings on both profiles, you can view each other's recent purchases, Wish Lists, upcoming birthdays, and e-mail address.

Adding someone as an Amazon friend can help you find people interested in networking or reviewing your product. To make an Amazon friend invitation, scroll about two-thirds of the way down your profile page, **www.Amazon.com/gp/pdp.** You'll see a heading for **Amazon Friends & Interesting People** and a search box where you can put in names or e-mail addresses. Clicking on the person's name or e-mail address allows you to send a message that will be forwarded by Amazon.

Amazon users have three options in responding to a friend invitation:

- **Accept** — Both members become each other's Amazon friend and appear on each other's list of Friends.

- **Decline** — The sender's invitation is removed from a list of pending invitations on the invitee's profile. The sender isn't notified the invitation is declined, and is free to send future invitations.

- **Decline and block** — Declines the invitation and prevents future Friends invitations. The sender's name appears in a "Blocked People" list visible to you on your profile, and you have the option of unblocking them later.

- **Ignore** — The default option, and probably the most popular. The recipient ignores the Friends invitation and deletes the e-mail.

Amazon users have the option of receiving friend invitations only from people who already know their e-mail address and enter it correctly into the invitation form. Here's how to manage this setting:

1. On your profile page, scroll down the middle column to the section labeled **Amazon Friends & Interesting People**.
2. Click **See your pending invitations**.
3. At the bottom, in the section labeled **Blocking Preference**, check the box **Block invitations from people who don't know my e-mail address** and click the yellow button **Save preferences**.

Interesting people

Amazon's Interesting People feature lets you bookmark users to easily view their latest Amazon activity—customer reviews, tagging activity, etc. To add someone to your interesting people list, go to their profile page and, in the box labeled **Your Actions**, click the link **Add to Interesting People**. You can search for people to add to your list by selecting **People** from the search pull-down menu at the top left corner of your profile page.

Advanced Amazon tools

Internet advertising can be a dicey proposition if you're selling inexpensive items or you have limited quantities. On the other hand, using *paid placements* can sometimes be an effective tactic if it delivers your message to your target audience. Since Amazon has such a large share of buyers in so many categories, it offers some of the best opportunities for showcasing your wares. A variety of items are eligible for Amazon's paid placement programs—books, music video, software, video games and software.

For an overview of Amazon's advertising programs, see:

http://www.amazon.com/Advertising

Buy X, Get Y

You can increase the odds of buyers finding your item by paying at least $750 a month to display it with a complementary item in Amazon's Buy X, Get Y program, known as BXGY. The primary benefit is that your product's name and a thumbnail image of it are prominently displayed on the detail page of a related item under the heading **Best Value**. Customers who buy both items get an additional 5 percent discount.

You'll pay more for a pairing with popular items. For example, Amazon charges $1,000 a month for pairing with a book with a sales rank of 1 to 250, and $750 a month for pairing with slower-selling books with ranks exceeding 250.

An ideal BXGY campaign would pair your item with Amazon's No. 1 bestseller in the same category, if that bestseller appealed precisely to your target market. The stronger the Amazon Sales Rank of the paired title, the more people will see your promotion, and the more traffic will be redirected to your item's detail page. But if the paired item isn't relevant to yours, it won't work. For example, pairing your book with an installment of *Harry Potter* might bring a ton of exposure, but it wouldn't produce many sales, unless your book appealed to precisely the same audience.

You can find BXGY candidates by browsing Amazon's category best-seller lists and searching Amazon for related keywords. Use the "Sort by" drop-down menu on the right to sift products according to sales rank, publication date, and price. You can also browse for potential pairings by visiting this link and clicking on the appropriate category:

http://www.amazon.com/gp/bestsellers

The main value of BXGY is sending readers to your item's detail page who might not find it otherwise. You can pair your item with only one other title at a time. Publishers can participate in BXGY under Amazon's "small vendor" program if they have less than $1 million in annual sales on Amazon by applying at:

http://www.Amazon.com/exec/obidos/subst/misc/co-op/small-vendor-faq.html

Weaknesses of BXGY

Amazon doesn't provide any figures on the success rates of BXGY promotions. Anecdotally, many users complain that while the program increases sales a bit, the revenue from those increased sales rarely covers the fees. However, BXGY is a tool used by some marketers to spark initial word of mouth for a product, and in that sense it can be considered an investment. Increasing your sales on Amazon often leads to more success because items with strong sales on Amazon appear higher in Amazon's recommendations. Amazon continually recommends additional products to buyers though notations on its Web site and in e-mails.

Often BXGY offers aren't compelling for buyers. Customers don't qualify for the program's 5 percent discount unless they purchase both the items new from Amazon; purchases of used copies don't count. For this reason, pairing your title with an older classic isn't effective if there's a plentiful supply of used or discounted copies. Buyers don't have much incentive to buy both items at full retail when they can get one deeply discounted.

Amazon offers more paid placement programs to large publishers, who can buy spots on Amazon's home page, category pages, and in specialized stores and seasonal lists such as "Back to School" or "Top Cookbooks of 2007." However, these placements aren't available under Amazon's Small Vendor program.

You can get BXGY-like exposure without paying fees if your sales are strong, relative to other items in your category. Amazon pairs your item with a related product in a display nearly identical to BXGY's **Best Value**, but in this case it's called **Better Together**.

To see this in action, go to any book's detail page on Amazon. Under the heading **Better Together**, you'll see the item paired with another book, much like BXGY, albeit without the extra 5 percent discount.

If you're selling a book that is the best-selling title in its niche, your item can appear on the Better-Together spot for several other related titles—another example of how strong sales on Amazon create more exposure for you.

Single New Product e-mails

Another Amazon placement opportunity used by publishers and manufacturers is Single New Product e-mails, or SNPs. Amazon sends e-mails announcing your new item to customers who've purchased similar things on Amazon before.

In the case of a book, for example, the publisher might suggest a list of ISBNs of complementary existing books. Amazon would develop a list of customers who had purchased the complementary books, and send them an e-mail announcing the new book being advertised. Amazon targets 5,000 to 10,000 recipients per mailing.

SNPs provide a unique marketing opportunity to marketers who don't have a large e-mail list of prospective buyers. The cost for small vendors with less than $1 million in annual sales on Amazon is $1,500 per title per SNP mailing. The item must be new—books are eligible for SNPs only during the 90 days following their publication date. To schedule SNPs, publishers must complete an SNP nomination form a few months before the publication date and commit to a certain month for the promotion.

Amapedia

Amazon's Amapedia feature (formerly called ProductWikis) enables customers to write their own articles, or "wikis," on any product page. The Amazon wikis resemble user-generated content popularized by Wikipedia.org, a free online encyclopedia. The feature was renamed Amapedia in 2007.

The concept behind wikis is that anyone can write one, and that anyone else can come along later and correct mistakes. Wikis are supposed to differ from customer reviews and other user-generated content in one important way: Writers are supposed to stick to facts, and avoid injecting their opinions.

What could undermine the utility of wikis is their misuse by spammers. And there's nothing to prevent competing authors or publishers from adding false information. Wikis are supposed to be self-correcting, but experience shows this doesn't always happen.

For more information, see:

http://amapedia.amazon.com

Customer Discussions

The "Customer Discussions" feature enables Amazon users to ask questions, share insights, and give opinions about products. One of the many possible uses of this feature might be to provide a forum for a manufacturer or seller to notify shoppers of a new product feature or other current information. You can subscribe to receive notifications from Amazon whenever new questions or responses are posted to a particular discussion.

To see the Customer Discussions for a particular item, scroll down the item detail page to the section **Customer Discussions.**

Pay-per-click advertising

Unlike with most advertising, with pay-per-click you don't pay fees each time your ad is displayed, but only when someone clicks on your ad and is taken to your Web site. PPC has revolutionized online promotion, and has been wonderfully effective for many Internet businesses. The prime advantage of PPC is its ability to deliver your ad to targeted audiences.

Although PPC can bring targeted traffic to your site, it's unlikely you'll convert enough of those visitors into immediate buyers unless you have unique, high-priced products or services. Google, for example, will charge you 75 cents or more per click for competitive keywords, and only a small fraction of those clicks will result in sales.

Google AdWords

With Google AdWords, advertisers write short three-line text ads, then bid on keywords relevant to their ad. The ads appear alongside relevant search results or on content pages. For example, to advertise your tropical fish store, you might bid on several different keywords and phrases—**aquarium**, **exotic fish**, **fishkeeping**, and **pet fish**. Depending on how popular those words and phrases are with other advertisers, you might have to pay a minimum of 10 cents, 30 cents, or several dollars for each click. The higher your bid, the higher your ad shows up on the relevant page.

You may, however, profit from PPC advertising if you take a long-term view. Do you know how much your customers are worth? If you get any repeat business at all, your customers are worth more than the profit margin from a single sale. If your average customer buys four items during the lifetime of their relationship with you—and your average net profit on those four items is $14 apiece—your average customer is worth $56.

If each of your customers is worth $56, would you spend a few dollars on advertising to attract more new customers?

The most familiar PPC ads are the ubiquitous Google "Sponsored Links" that appear alongside search results or on content-related websites.

Businesses that use PPC ads target their customers by bidding on keywords related to what they're selling. For example, if you're selling scuba-diving equipment, you might bid on the keywords **snorkeling** or **diving**. If you bid sufficiently high, your ad will appear on relevant Web sites when someone searches for your keyword. You pay for the ad only when someone clicks on it, and the more popular the keyword, the more you'll pay. An obscure keyword might be available for a nickel per click on some networks, while a highly competitive keyword might cost as much as $50 per click.

Learn more about Google's AdWords program at:

http://adwords.google.com

Until recent years, Google AdWords and Yahoo Search Marketing were practically the only alternatives for PPC, with Google commanding a lion's share of the market. Back then PPC was often called "search engine advertising" because ads were always displayed alongside search results at Google, Yahoo, or another search engine. Sometimes the only thing differentiating your ad from a natural (or organic) search result was the small label "Sponsored Link."

PPC was viewed as a revolutionary way of advertising because you spent money to attract people who had already expressed an interest in what you were selling. In the past couple of years, Google seems to have perfected PPC with its AdWords program. Not only are ads shown alongside search results, but they also pop up on millions of Web sites—relevant blogs, commerce sites, forums, etc. Meanwhile, Amazon has launched its own PPC program.

Clickriver/Amazon Product Ads

Because advertisers have driven up the bidding on many popular PPC keywords, PPC isn't a particularly effective way to sell individual low-priced items with Google Adwords. A newer opportunity exists with Amazon's PPC networks, Clickriver and Product Ads. Amazon permits advertisements only for services on Clickriver, product marketers must use Amazon Product Ads.

Clickriver displays ads on its product detail pages and can be used to direct traffic to your own Web site or anywhere else. One obvious advantage with Amazon's ad network is that it reaches Amazon's millions of registered online buyers. The plain-text ads appear about halfway down product detail pages under the heading "Customers viewing this page may be interested in these Sponsored Links."

First, the good news: Clickriver is much easier to use than Google AdWords. The interface is clean and it responds quickly. If you ask for a keyword, your ads begin appearing within seconds. It's also relatively cheap compared with Google because many keywords cost just 10 cents per click. Perhaps the low prices indicate that not many advertisers are competing for the keywords, at least not yet.

Clickriver does a great job of suggesting additional keywords. For example, let's imagine you're advertising a landscaping service. Once Clickriver knows you're targeting landscaping customers, it will suggest every book title and author name in that topic, at least those with good sales records. This helps you get your ad in front of the right people. It sounds obvious, but you'd be surprised how many good keywords Clickriver will suggest that you didn't think of.

Keywords aren't the only prospecting tool on Clickriver. You can also target entire categories in Amazon's bookstore in one fell swoop. For example, if you wanted your ad to appear on all Amazon book pages related to "gardening," you'd create a new ad and use the keywords "category gardening."

And now, the bad news: Clicks are very, very sparse with Clickriver. It's very likely that the low click-through rate is because Clickriver ads just aren't that visible on Amazon's detail pages. Visibility will probably always be a tension for this program: For the ads to be more effective,

Amazon would need to raise their profile. But that might distract buyers from buying the thing they were originally viewing on Amazon.

Amazon Product Ads

Product Ads is a newer Amazon pay-pay-click program that displays links to product pages on other Web sites. By participating in this program, you can add products on Amazon.com and create links to your Web site. Advertisers bid against one another for space in the Amazon category where they want their ads to appear. The higher you bid, the more exposure your ads receive.

Your links may appear on product detail pages, or in search results. Customers who click on the links are forwarded to your Web site.

One convenient feature with Product Ads is that you can upload a list of the products you want to promote, instead of manually creating an ad for each product.

Product Ads may be displayed in these categories: Electronics & Computers, Home & Garden, Tools, and Toys, Kids & Baby. For more information, see:

http://www.amazonservices.com/productAds/

The future of PPC

Like many other Internet tools, PPC is evolving at a breakneck pace. So far in this section, we've examined only "keyword-based" PPC systems. But there's a whole other world of PPC that can work for online marketers, known as "product PPC" or "price comparison PPC." Some well-known examples of these are Shopzilla.com, NexTag.com, Biz-Rate.com, Shopping.com, and PriceGrabber.com. It works like this: Participating advertisers upload a list of their inventory. When visitors search for a product, the links to various advertisers show up. Advertisers who pay more are given prominence, but users can also sort the listings to find the lowest price. Each time a visitor buys, the advertiser pays a fee.

It's likely that the competition for PPC advertisers will heat up significantly in the future. Microsoft is also getting into the act, beta-testing a PPC network called MSN adCenter.

Your own Web site

Even if your main business is selling items on Amazon, you shouldn't overlook the potential profits of augmenting that business with your own Web site. One simple way to do this is to open a WebStore, an e-commerce site hosted by Amazon but with your own branding. Using a WebStore, you can offer your own merchandise directly to shoppers on your own Web site while simultaneously earning commissions on sales of items from other merchants you feature in your store. You can display your inventory anywhere you wish—on Amazon, only in your WebStore, or in both places.

Currently Amazon charges $59.99 and takes a 7 percent commission on the sales of your items. It's a hefty fee, but it brings access to Amazon's registered buyers, who can easily use their existing Amazon account to buy your products. In effect, you're piggybacking on Amazon's brand and reputation for customer service. Amazon calls the 7 percent it takes a "commission," and all payment-processing fees are included, so you don't need to use a service like PayPal or a credit-card merchant account.

WebStore includes credit-card processing, fraud protection, and built-in search engine marketing services. There are no surprise fees sometimes found with other store providers, such as hosting, payment gateways or merchant accounts. Also, your buyers are covered by the same A-to-Z Guarantee provided when shopping directly at Amazon.com.

After you open a WebStore account, you get a link from Amazon to your WebStore, and Amazon exports feeds of your products to help your items show up in search results on Google and other search engines. Amazon also provides a site map, which helps your WebStore visibility by getting properly indexed by the search engines. You can also add various affiliate and advertising programs, such as Google Adsense, to your WebStore to generate additional revenue.

The WebStore is a good way for someone with a blog or content Web site to generate revenue from visitors. By adding a WebStore to your existing site, you automatically add Amazon's extensive merchandising and community features like customer reviews and bestseller lists.

When items offered by Amazon or other merchants are sold through your WebStore, you earn a commission through the company's affiliate program, known as **Amazon Associates**, which is explained later in this book.

To take a tour of WebStore's features, see:

http://webstore.amazon.com

WebStore features

- Set up an initial Web site in minutes with a "1-Click Web-Store" feature.

- Create multiple stores on multiple domains but pay just one monthly fee. You can create different sites or "micro-sites" dedicated to separate brands, categories or offers.

- Adjust the look and feel of your WebStore using Amazon's online tools, no computer coding required.

- Use integrated e-mail campaign-management software for marketing to your customers.

- Attract new customers through built-in search engine marketing services directly through your WebStore interface.

- Customize meta tags for your content and category pages.

- Easily add Google Analytics code and a Google Sitemap.

- Manage page redirects (301 redirects) from your old store to your new WebStore so your pages continue to be indexed by search engines.

You can list an unlimited number of products in your WebStore, and the $59.99 monthly fee stays the same. Your store has the same shopping cart and technology that Amazon customers are comfortable with.

Remember, though, your WebStore doesn't have any exposure on Amazon itself. In other words, your WebStore listings won't show up in Amazon searches, so you have to market the WebStore and generate your own traffic. On the other hand, your WebStore isn't competing directly against other sellers, as happens on Amazon Marketplace.

Another advantage of an Amazon WebStore is the relative ease in uploading your product inventory. You'll have access to Amazon's Web-based tool and a downloadable desktop application to upload your entire catalog.

You can point your existing domain name at your WebStore. If you don't have a domain name, your store will appear at an Amazon-provided URL. You can also purchase a new domain name for your WebStore from any domain name registrar. You may integrate your WebStore with Amazon's Pro-Merchant or Fulfillment by Amazon programs.

After designing your WebStore, you can preview and publish it to a temporary site automatically generated by Amazon or you can publish your store to your existing domain.

If you'd like Amazon to assist you with professional design or search engine marketing services, send an e-mail to webstore-dcp@amazon.com.

Manage your WebStore

Redirecting your domain name. You can use either of two options for navigation to your WebStore by using your existing domain name. One, you can configure the settings yourself using instructions from Amazon. Secondly, you can contact your domain registrar and ask them to complete the domain name configuration for you. Detailed steps for each option appear in the complete WebStore documentation you receive after registration.

Managing WebStore orders. You can receive notification of orders via e-mail, feed or by viewing your Seller Central account on the Web. Orders appear under the **Orders** tab in Seller Central, allowing you to distinguish them from Amazon.com orders, if you also have an Amazon merchant account. You can search and sort orders and issue refunds.

Customer feedback and reviews. By default, your WebStore will display customer reviews for products sold on Amazon.com. So if you have a long, positive track record at Amazon regarding customer satisfaction, this will be a big advantage for your WebStore. Customers at your WebStore can submit feedback on a transaction, just as they can at Marketplace. However, you can turn off the feedback display at your WebStore if you wish. Also, you have the option of allowing customers to write product reviews on your WebStore site and feedback for any order, regardless of whether it originated on Amazon.com or your WebStore.

Promotion management. You can make special offers on your WebStore products. According to the merchant program you participate in, you can offer:

- Fixed Amount Off
- Percentage off
- Free Shipping
- Free Product
- Evaluation Group
- Customized promotion message on the product detail page
- Cheapest of all, Cheapest of every N, Average Price

If you sell on Amazon and have a WebStore too, your promotions will appear on both venues.

Other e-commerce hosts

Amazon's WebStores aren't your only choice for hosting your own online store. You can review a multitude of affordable options for store hosting simply by searching the Web for "store hosting." Vendio is just one example of a vendor who can host your store on the Internet:

http://www.vendio.com/services/stores.html

- **eBay ProStores.** eBay also offers independent merchants a store hosting solution through its ProStores unit, which serves small- and medium-sized businesses. ProStores provides a customizable online storefront, allowing you to use your own Web address instead of your eBay URL. ProStores provides domain registration and hosting, a shopping cart function, and credit card processing. Three levels of service are offered, with fees ranging from $29.95 to $249.95 per month. For more information, see:

http://www.prostores.com/

Earn side revenue

In addition to the sales you can make on your site—whether it's a WebStore, a blog, or virtually any other type of site—the visitors provide additional income opportunities if you join the right affiliate programs and take advantage of the advertising opportunities. If your site becomes extremely popular, the revenue could be substantial.

New sites usually generate negligible revenue, but advertising or affiliate programs can still be worthwhile. Your audience may appreciate niche advertising, and these programs can boost your visibility with search engines. One option is to donate your affiliate and ad revenues to charities admired by your audience, which sometimes can be handled automatically. The public-relations benefit of donating could outweigh the monetary value, and you won't have to account for it as income and pay tax on it.

Here are some of the most popular advertising and affiliate programs merchants can use on their Web sites:

- **Amazon Associates.** Amazon's affiliate program is called Amazon Associates. You can display links for your product and related ones on Amazon. When your visitors click through to Amazon and make a purchase, you're paid a commission. Typically your commission is a few percentage points of the total sale, depending on the type of merchandise.

Amazon Associates is one of the most familiar and successful programs on the Internet, with more than 1 million member sites. After joining you receive an Associates ID code, which you insert into your links to Amazon products.

After your visitors click on your Associates link, you'll receive commissions on most other purchases those customers make during the following 24 hours. For example, if your visitor buys a plasma TV on Amazon during that same 24-hour session, you'll get a commission.

In 2006 Amazon Associates introduced a new contextual program called Omakase, which displays different products based on the content on your site and your visitor's browsing history at Amazon. The advantage for affiliates is that Omakase is dynamic, exposing your audience to different products each time they visit a different page on your site, increasing the odds of a purchase.

The name Omakase is Japanese for "Leave it up to us," a custom in Japanese restaurants in which the chef improvises a meal based on his knowledge of the diner's preferences.

Commission Junction. Opening an account at Commission Junction provides access to hundreds of niche affiliate programs. You'll find affiliate opportunities for nearly any type of product, including dozens of specialized retailers. The site provides the codes you'll need to insert on your Web site, and consolidated reports of your commissions. See:

http://www.CommissionJunction.com

eBay. If there's a category of merchandise on eBay of interest to your target market, open an affiliate account. You can display relevant ads for popular auctions on your site. According to eBay, its top 25 affiliates average more than $100,000 in commissions every month.

The ads contain product information, gallery images, bidding prices, and ending times. eBay claims that the click-through rates for these ads are double that of regular banner ads.

eBay sellers may earn commissions from sending traffic to their own listings or to listings of other sellers. Using eBay's affiliate Editor's Kit, sellers can display their own listings on a Web site or blog, and they can cross-promote items from other sellers and earn commissions on all resulting sales.

After joining, you can operate your eBay affiliate account through the Commission Junction service, mentioned above. For more information, see:

http://affiliates.ebay.com

Amazon aStores

aStore is a product allowing any Amazon affiliate (a member of the Amazon Associates program) to create a professional-looking online store in just a few minutes without any programming skills. Your aStore can be embedded within your own Web site, or you can link to an external aStore.

aStore's setup tool guides you through the steps and generates a URL for your store. There's no fee for having an aStore, and your affiliate commissions are handled just like other Associates links. You can build up to 100 aStores with the same Associates account.

Here are some of the more notable features of aStores:

- **Access all categories.** You have access to every Amazon.com category and subcategory for automatically populating your product categories. If Amazon has created a group for it, such as Biographies of John F. Kennedy, you can create a category page to automatically pull in those products and organize these categories however you wish.

- **Unlimited category/subcategory nesting.** You can create as many levels of product categories and subcategories as you wish, and populate the products in each category by Amazon bestsellers, hand-picking them, or importing a Listmania list.

- **Build your own category navigation.** Advanced users can take integration with their existing Web sites a step further by hiding the aStore category navigation and building their own directly within the core site navigation.

The TypePad bookstore, an example of an aStore that integrates a primary Web site with an aStore by selecting and categorizing products related to its content. aStore's color and design tools were used to match the look and feel of the Web site.

- **CSS control.** Advanced users can directly edit the stylesheets for their stores, and share those with others.

- **aStore Widgets.** You can advertise your store to your site visitors using these banner links, increasing your aStore traffic.

For more information, see:

http://www.Amazon.com/associates

Google AdSense. Google's AdSense program is perhaps the best-known Web ad network, and it's relatively easy to sign up and incorporate text or banner ads onto your site. For more information, see:

www.Google.com/Adsense

Two alternatives to AdSense are **www.AdBrite.com** and **www.BlogAds.com**.

Amazon Advantage

Amazon's Advantage program is the company's inventory consignment program for small and midsize publishers of books, and music and videos published as CDs or DVDs. With Advantage, publishers ship their items to Amazon's warehouse at their expense. Amazon sells the merchandise on its site and handles all the customer service and shipping.

Amazon Advantage offers two advantages that are especially compelling for small publishers who don't otherwise have access to retail channels or a distributor:

- It provides your product with the same exposure as titles from other publishers having wide distribution and big marketing budgets.

- Amazon shows your title as available for "one-day shipping," and offers free shipping to buyers in many cases, which can boost sales.

These advantages, however, don't come cheap for the publisher. Advantage members must give Amazon a wholesale discount of 55 percent. That means if your title's suggested retail price is $20, Amazon takes $11 on each sale, and you take $9. And don't forget, out of your $9 you must pay for the production of each item and shipping it to Amazon's warehouse.

You, the publisher, set the list price, also known as the "suggested retail price." Although Amazon is entitled to 55 percent of that amount, it often offers buyers a discount from that price. For example, books with a list price of $19.95 are often offered at $13.57 (32 percent off list).

In this case, the customer's discount comes from Amazon's take. In other words, Amazon is reducing its profit to give the customer a better deal. The publisher is still getting his original wholesale price, which is 45 percent of list.

If your title is enrolled in Advantage, it will also appear for sale on other Web sites such as Borders.com, Target.com, VirginMega.com and Waldenbooks.com.

To enroll in Advantage, you must retain the North American distribution rights for your title, and it must have a scannable barcode and valid ISBN. If you do not have an ISBN, you can purchase them in sets of 10 for $225 from the U.S. ISBN Agency:

http://www.isbn.org

You can apply online for the Advantage Program and submit your titles for consideration. If approved, you'll list your items in Amazon's catalog, provide descriptive content, and ship books to an Amazon warehouse. When a customer purchases your title, Amazon processes the order within 24 hours. Amazon tracks your inventory and sends e-mail requests for you to ship more copies to their warehouse based on customer demand. For your previous month's sales, Amazon deposits money into your checking account via electronic funds transfer.

To apply for Advantage, visit this page:

http://advantage.amazon.com/gp/vendor/public/join

It's important to remember that Advantage is a consignment sales model; you're not earning money when you ship your titles to Amazon. Payments are made for sold units at the end of the following month. In other words, if a copy sells during March, you'll get paid by Amazon on the last day of April.

Advantage vs. Fulfillment by Amazon

Unlike with the Fulfillment by Amazon program, no merchant account is required for Amazon Advantage, and publishers are charged no storage fees for items they store in Amazon's warehouse. However, unlike with FBA, Advantage users have no control over how many of their items Amazon stocks.

Here is a cost comparison of the two programs, Amazon Advantage, and Fulfillment by Amazon:

	Advantage	FBA
Program Fees	$29.95/year	$39.95/month*

Book Example	Advantage	FBA
2 lb Book Price	$ 25.00	$ 25.00
Sales commission	$ 13.75	$ 3.75
Sales fees	$ -	$ 1.20
Fulfillment fees	$ -	$ 1.80
Storage fees**	$ -	$ 0.05
Net to seller	$ 11.25	$ 18.20

CD Example	Advantage	FBA
2 lb CD Set	$ 18.00	$ 18.00
Sales commission	$ 9.90	$ 2.70
Sales fees	$ -	$ 0.70
Fulfillment fees	$ -	$ 1.30
Storage fees**	$ -	$ 0.05
Net to seller	$ 8.10	$ 13.25

* Pro Merchant sellers can create new items in the Amazon catalog, and do not pay the "seller closing fee" of $0.99/transaction.

**Advantage items are limited by the amount of inventory that can be stored; FBA storage fee is calculated nightly and charged monthly.

Manage the details

As an Advantage member, you'll be able to manage the detail page content for all your titles. You'll be able to upload bibliographic data, descriptions, editorial reviews, and artwork.

Advantage also provides online sales and inventory reports. The reports, updated daily, show:

- Unit sales last month.

- Unit sales this month.

- Current inventory.

- Status of the last order that Amazon.com placed with you to re-plenish our inventory.

- Amount of your next payment.

Advantage Professional

Amazon offers different terms for publishers of certain high-priced, specialized books. The Advantage Professional program is often suitable for:

- Publishers of higher-priced professional, technical, and medical books.

- Providers of educational DVDs, videos, or CDs that are scholarly, professional, or technical in nature, and not widely available through normal retail channels.

- Non-profit (501(c)3) groups.

Advantage Professional is nearly identical to the regular Advantage program except that it offers more flexibility on discount rates. To be eligible for the program, publishers must enroll five or more qualified titles that sell for at least $35 per unit. Self-help and How-to titles aren't considered for Advantage Professional.

To enroll in Advantage Professional, complete the survey here:

http://advantage.amazon.com/gp/vendor/public/professional

Each book title must have a valid ISBN. Video and music products must have an ISBN or an EAN printed on the back of each copy, along with a corresponding barcode. If the product is shrink-wrapped or otherwise encased, the barcode must be scannable from the other package. Non-scannable items may incur an extra handling fee or be returned at your cost.

Index